D0442007

ALL NEW
SQUARE
FOOT
GARDENING
Cookbook

Published by Cool Springs Press
P.O. Box 2828
Brentwood, Tennessee 37024

Bartholomew, Mel.
All new square foot gardening cookbook : [taking the harvest to the table] / Mel Bartholomew.
p. cm.
Includes index.
ISBN 978-1-59186-459-2
1. Cookery (Vegetables) 2. Cookery (Fruit) 3. Cookery (Herbs) I. Title.

TX801.B317 2009
641.6'51--dc22

2009042416

EAN: 978-1-59186-459-2

First Printing 2009
Printed in the United States of America
10 9 8 7 6 5 4 3 2 1

Editor: Nicki Pendleton Wood
Art Director: Marc Pewitt
Research Assistant: Lori Pelkowski

On the Cover: Mel Bartholomew, photographed by Ed Rode

Special thanks to "Babs" Freeman for opening her home and garden to Mel and the staff of Cool Springs Press.

PHOTOGRAPHY
The following photos are © as indicated / Fotolia
page 19 roast asparagus © Superfood; page 21 asparagus frittata © Mario; page 29 © robynmac; page 31 © EuToch; page 37 © JJAVA; page 39 © Jaroslaw Grudzinski; page 45 © nettestock; page 47 © JJAVA; page 53, © David Smith; page 55 © Robert Lerich; page 61 © Maria Brzostowska; page 63 © Mnkey Business; page 69 © kunstlichtstudio; page 71 © Lechatmachine; page 79 © pitrs; page 85 © Edie Layland; page 87 © Jaimie Duplass; page 95 © vaso; page 97 © Ashley Whitworth; page 103 © Monkey Business; page 105 © Kasia Biel; page 115 © Fiona Mark; page 119 © William Berry; page 121 © Dragan Veselinov; page 129 © Silvia Bogdanski; page 131 © Sergejs Rahunoks; page 137 © vlas2002; page 139 © monamakela.com; page 145 © vphoto; page 147 © Comugnero Silvana; page 155 © Katarzyna Malecka; page 157 © Victoria P.

Ed Rode: 5, 7, 8, 9, 11, 13, 14, 17, 76, 92, 110, 116, 125, 152, 162, 176

Jupiter Images: 16, 24, 26, 27, 34, 42, 50, 58, 66, 74, 82, 100, 108, 113, 126

iStockphoto and its artists: 133, 142

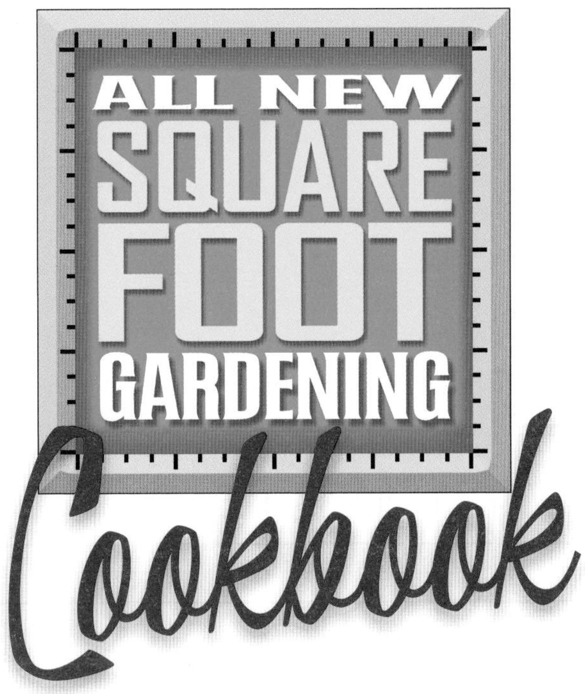

Mel Bartholomew

Growing Successful Gardeners™

www.coolspringspress.com

BRENTWOOD, TENNESSEE

Dedication

To all you loyal Square Foot Gardening fans who have found a new way to garden and now want to enjoy a healthy way of eating all those good things from your Square Foot garden.

Contents

Dedication....................4

Foreword....................8

Welcome to Square Foot Cooking!....................12

Fruit & Vegetables

ASPARAGUS....................16

BEANS....................24

BROCCOLI....................34

CABBAGE....................42

CARROTS....................50

CUCUMBERS....................58

EGGPLANT....................66

HERBS....................74

SALAD GREENS....................82

MELONS & BERRIES....................92

PEAS....................100

ONIONS, GARLIC & CHIVES....................108

PEPPERS....................116

POTATOES....................126

CHARD & FRIENDS....................134

SQUASHES....................142

TOMATOES....................152

Appendix....................162

Planting Grids

Planting Schedules

Index....................170

Meet Mel Bartholomew....................176

Foreword

Place your palms together and spread your fingers. Now fold them together: that effortless interlacing is how I think of Square Foot Gardening. All parts of the Square Foot garden, from the approach to the end, the form and function, weave together into a system.

At the center is the goal of efficiency, growing the most food of the best quality in the smallest space with no superfluous effort. Square Foot Gardening is a more efficient use of land, energy, and water than traditional row gardening. The 48-inch-square boxes and three-foot paths are based on the human reach. The closely spaced squares minimize the opportunity for weeds and therefore, the need for weeding. Then there's the health benefit. A garden produces fresh fruits and vegetables that form the center of a healthful way of eating. A garden brings people out of doors and into the sunshine and fresh air, for some simple, healthful movement that almost anyone with basic mobility can perform. The method produces the most from the smallest amount of land, particularly if you follow the seed-starting and planting charts in *All New Square Foot Gardening*. As early-season vegetables complete their growing cycle, you'll have plants ready to replace them, ensuring a steady supply of fresh produce. If you're persistent and determined, each four-foot square can produce enough

food for one person for a year.

And there's the environmental effect of a Square Foot garden. You see how a garden free from toxic chemicals buzzes with beneficial insects and attracts delightful creatures. Homegrown vegetables mean fewer industrial farms, which mean less fertilizer runoff. And your prepared "Mel's Mix" soil means there's no need to fertilize, so you save that money and effort, and eliminate stream pollution. A Square Foot garden will save you trips to the supermarket. The smaller space means less watering and less water waste.

The efficiencies continue when you get to the kitchen. To me, the most efficient way to eat vegetables is fresh and uncooked. There's no heat involved, so it conserves energy. Uncooked vegetables retain all their nutrients. And your energy is conserved, too, when dinner involves merely selecting your food, cleaning it, and eating it.

My own garden emphasizes salad-type foods that can be eaten fresh, with a minimum of preparation. As a bonus, there's very little clean-up or dishwashing involved.

You'll make the planting, harvesting, and meal-planning decisions that work for your household, but I encourage you to try growing as much as you can in your plot, and to enjoy your fresh harvest for the sun-warmed, garden-fresh, peak-of-ripeness flavor that you just won't get with commercially grown, store-bought fruits and vegetables.

To help you maximize the good taste of your garden's good things, we've selected 135 recipes using 17 popular kitchen garden plants. The cookbook is arranged alphabetically by plant. Each section includes a harvest and yield guide, to give you an idea of what to expect from each plant, along with advice on the best way to gather the vegetables and fruits.

Where applicable, we've included a recipe in each section to deal with bumper crops, including sauces and simple pickles. And where it's practical, we've included a recipe to make the most of "overgrown" vegetables that have matured past the tender stage.

Each chapter includes a Kid's Corner idea to encourage the interest of children and grandchildren, not only to have their own Square Foot garden, but to get the most out of them by creating fun activities, as well as learning something new and different. This is something they will use the rest of their lives.

Finally, there's the spiritual side of a garden. Growing your own food helps develop a reverence for the processes of nature. A crown of broccoli becomes more magical when you can see the marvelous combination of chemistry, meteorology, botany, and all that produce it. In a garden, you can see for yourself, and show children, what the seasons are, and what a celebration each newly ripened vegetable represents. Gardening develops a reverence for the earth, and with it, a special sense of responsibility.

Square Foot Gardening makes all this magic happen in a small space. And all these good results come from caring for one small square of the earth—yours.

Learn more and find other Square Foot Gardening enthusiasts at www.squarefootgardening.com. You'll also find information and answers to the most common Square Foot Gardening questions, regional gardening forums where you can chat with fellow gardeners, and a selection of books and gardening supplies to bring your garden to its peak of productivity and health.

—Mel Bartholomew

Welcome to Square Foot Cooking!

In the late winter of 2009, for the first time in years, I'd begun a backyard kitchen garden that would become the year's destiny.

But it didn't look that way in the gray days of February. The garden spot was tilled up but nothing was planted. I was selecting seeds, deciding on plants. The previous two years, our weekly box from a farm garden program supplied lots of what we didn't want so I tried to figure out how to grow more of what we liked and less of what we didn't.

On precisely the day I planned to set out rows of plants, I was offered the opportunity to work with Mel Bartholomew on the *All New Square Foot Gardening Cookbook*. In one afternoon, I read his book on Square Foot Gardening and transformed a plowed garden into a Square Foot garden. His logic was undeniable, and the method itself was intuitive. Not rows but squares. No need to commit to a whole row of peas or fennel or chard—just try a little. I called it the "chocolate box" approach. No big commitment, just lots of nice little things. A bit of this and a bit of that.

Within a couple of weeks, there were lettuce and arugula. So the salad chapter developed and was tried and tested. Chives, thyme, chervil, burnett, lovage, and chard came next, and the earliest little cucumbers. The herbs, greens, and cucumber chapters were developed. The first green beans, the early banana peppers, a single zucchini. The chapters suggested themselves as the garden abounded with good things.

That was in late May, and from then forward, all our vegetables came from our garden, save for early garlic and onions, lemons for salad dressing, a watermelon for July 4, and local peaches.

Growing the garden was important in developing the recipes for the *All New Square Foot Gardening Cookbook*. A Square Foot garden abounds with produce, which arrives in dollops rather than all at once. That fact helped shape the recipes, and you'll find plenty of recipes that use just a handful of beans, just a single zucchini, or just one cucumber.

Similarly, you never know until you walk into the garden quite what will be ready for picking. That led to flexible recipes that can be prepared with any of several different vegetables. A sauté of beans will also work with chard. A zucchini pancake can instead be made with steamed spinach or grated carrots. If you don't have the sugar snaps that a recipe calls for, regular peas or tender green beans are a brilliant substitute.

The garden itself also demanded a re-scaling of recipes. Many recipes from ordinary cookbooks call for more than a pound of cabbage, asparagus, or spinach,

which would be an unusually large one-time harvest from an average backyard Square Foot garden. The recipes are scaled to require less than one pound of a vegetable, an amount you can often pick in the span of two to three days.

In keeping with Mel's philosophy of eating fresh and uncooked foods, each chapter (where practical) offers a few fresh and uncooked uses for vegetables. (But not squash and potatoes—though if you try that, please visit the forums at www.squarefootgardening.com and share your experience.) Even in a well-planned and tightly scheduled Square Foot garden, you will occasionally find the vegetable bins bulging with squash, peppers, or beans, when the family is weary of squash, peppers, and beans. Look for a pickling, sauce, or other recipe in many of the chapters to help preserve the good things for later in the year.

My gardening and kitchen life have been so enriched by that one chance day in spring 2009. I can feel delighted, sustainable, and self-sufficient about the food I put on the table. You can, too, and it's so simple you'll want to spread the word.

—Nicki Pendleton Wood
Editor

Nicki Pendleton Wood is a food writer, cookbook editor and food blogger in Nashville, Tennessee.

ALL NEW
SQUARE
FOOT
GARDENING
Cookbook

Taking the Harvest to the Table

Asparagus

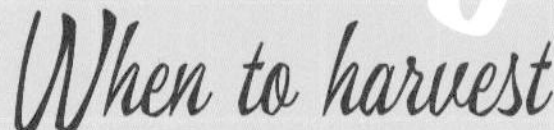

When to harvest

Harvest all shoots at 3/8-inch (finger size) diameter for best flavor. As they are harvested, the next shoots will get smaller. When there are no more shoots larger than 3/8 inch, stop harvesting and let the rest grow. An established three-year-old asparagus bed can produce edible spears for up to six weeks.

Signs that it is ready

Harvest the spears when they are eight inches above the ground, before the scales on the tips start to open.

When is it too late?

When all the new shoots are smaller than 3/8 inch in diameter, or the tops start opening, leave them on the plant to help feed the roots.

How to harvest

To pick asparagus, snap the spear by hand. It should break off at just the right place. Above tender, below that breaking point not so tender. Or you can cut each spear at soil level with a sharp knife, trying not to cut the other shoots nearby. Then try the bend-and-break action to find the tenderest point.

Expected yield

Plant one root system (called a "crown") per square foot to start. The patch will grow into a good stand of stalks in two to three years. Each mature plant will produce from three to six harvestable stalks per plant in spring.

TIPS

KID'S CORNER

Combine economics with farming or gardening by doing a price comparison of asparagus. Keep a record of how much the plant costs, or check at a garden center. Estimate dollars per month for the land, water, and weeding. How much is a bunch of asparagus at the market? And how much did your homegrown asparagus cost?

- *Storage*
  Store fresh asparagus in the refrigerator by first breaking off the large end of each spear where it snaps easily. Then wrap the bottom of the stalks in a damp paper towel and put them in a plastic bag. Plan to use them within two days. You can also refrigerate asparagus standing upright in a container that has a couple of inches of cold water in the bottom. Then put a plastic bag loosely around the tops. They will last three or four days this way. You can also freeze or pickle asparagus.

- *Eat / Don't Eat*
  The young, finger-size shoots are edible when they reach about eight inches long.

- *Companion Planting*
  Parsley and basil; tomatoes can deter asparagus beetles.

- *This 'n' That*
  In Greece, Italy, and France, asparagus is harvested in the wild and chopped into omelets.

Mel says...

Very thin asparagus, thinner than a pencil, is slightly stringier than spears that have matured for another day or two, the opposite of what you'd expect. So for asparagus that's more tender and juicy, leave them in the ground for a couple of days.

Roasted Asparagus with Cherry Tomatoes

Roasting brings out the sweetness of vegetables, while the basil adds a whiff of herbs.

8 asparagus spears, trimmed
10 cherry tomatoes
8 kalamata or other cured black olives, pitted, optional
2 tablespoons olive oil
1 garlic clove, thinly sliced
8 basil leaves
Salt and freshly ground pepper to taste

Preheat the oven to 425 degrees. Combine the asparagus, tomatoes, olives, oil, garlic, basil, salt and pepper in a large bowl and mix well. Spread in a single layer in a roasting pan. Roast for 12 minutes, stirring and turning twice. Makes 2 to 3 servings.

Asparagus Wild Rice Salad

You can customize this salad to your taste with either Asian or Italian flavors. The Asian version uses watercress, cilantro, and a Sesame Ginger Vinaigrette. The Italian version uses arugula, parsley, and Rosemary Lemon Vinaigrette.

2 cups cooked wild rice, or wild and white blend, cooled
6 to 10 asparagus spears
1 cup chopped watercress or torn young arugula
2 tablespoons chopped fresh cilantro or parsley
Sesame Ginger Vinaigrette (page 23) or Rosemary Lemon Vinaigrette (page 22)
Salt and freshly ground pepper to taste

Combine the rice, asparagus, watercress and cilantro in a medium serving bowl. Add about ½ cup dressing and mix well. Season with additional salt and pepper. Makes 6 servings.

Roasted Asparagus with Cherry Tomatoes

Asparagus Frittata

Fresh herbs add the top note of flavor to this light meal.

- 2 garlic cloves, minced
- 1 tablespoon olive oil
- 16 thin asparagus, trimmed, cut into 1-inch lengths
- 3 eggs
- 1 tablespoon snipped fresh chives
- 2 tablespoons minced fresh parsley
- Salt and freshly ground pepper to taste

Preheat the broiler. Sauté the garlic in the olive oil in an 8- to 10-inch nonstick skillet over low heat until fragrant. Add the asparagus and sauté for 3 minutes until it begins to soften.

Beat the eggs, chives, salt and pepper in a bowl until well blended. Pour over the asparagus in the skillet, tilting to coat the bottom of the skillet evenly with the egg mixture. Cover the pan and cook for 1 to 2 minutes until the frittata is set on the bottom. Uncover the pan and place under the broiler for 1 minute until center is set. Sprinkle with parsley. Serve hot or at room temperature. Makes 3 servings.

Brunch Asparagus Pick-Ups

These look pretty and are easy to eat standing at a party.

- 16 asparagus spears
- 1 (8-count) package refrigerated crescent rolls
- 1 cup grated mild white cheese such as Muenster or Monterey Jack
- 4 bacon slices, crisp-cooked and crumbled, optional
- 3 green onions, sliced

Preheat the oven to 400 degrees. Snap the woody ends off the asparagus spears by bending them; they will naturally break at the proper place. Boil in 2 inches of water, steam, or microsteam for 2 to 7 minutes until tender-crisp; drain. Pat the asparagus dry, and keep them wrapped in a clean kitchen towel or paper towel to absorb as much water as possible.

Separate the dough into 8 triangles. Divide the cheese, bacon and green onions among the rolls, leaving a border so the ingredients don't come out of the roll as it bakes. Place two asparagus spears on the wide end of each triangle. Roll to enclose all ingredients.

Arrange the rolls on a greased baking sheet. Bake for 10 to 12 minutes until the rolls are browned. Makes 8 servings.

Asparagus Frittata

Fresh Asparagus Snow Pea Slaw

Fresh ingredients just need a little lemon juice, oil and your homegrown herbs.

Rosemary Lemon Vinaigrette
½ cup olive oil
½ cup canola oil
1 teaspoon Dijon mustard
Zest and juice of 1 lemon
1 teaspoon fresh rosemary leaves
1 tablespoon white wine vinegar
Salt and freshly ground pepper to taste

Slaw
10 asparagus spears
1 cup snow peas or sugar snaps
1 large carrot
4 green onions
10 basil leaves

For the dressing, combine the olive oil, canola oil, mustard, lemon zest and juice, rosemary, vinegar, salt and pepper in a bowl with a whisk or fork; mix well.

Snap the woody ends off the asparagus spears by bending them; they will naturally break at the proper place. Cut the asparagus into ½-inch pieces. Cut the sugar snaps into pieces. Cut the carrot into thirds. Cut each third into thirds longwise. Stack the slices and cut into matchsticks. Snip or slice the green onions. Stack three or four basil leaves, then roll into a cigar shape. Cut off slices to form ribbons of basil.

Combine all the ingredients in a medium serving bowl. Toss to coat with dressing. Makes 4 servings.

Grilled Asparagus

For a meal from the grill, start grilling a flat-iron or flank steak a few minutes before starting the asparagus. Slice the steak and serve the asparagus and steak over a salad tossed with vinaigrette, or over rice for a bigger appetite.

1 pound asparagus spears
2 tablespoons vegetable oil or olive oil
Coarse salt to taste

Prepare a low fire in the grill. Combine the asparagus, oil and salt in a shallow dish or plastic bag and stir or shake to coat. Arrange the asparagus individually on the grill, or use a grill wok or grill basket. For distinctive grill marks, grill over the low fire without moving the asparagus for about 2 minutes until they are half cooked. Turn the asparagus, stir in the wok, or shake the basket. Grill for 1 to 2 minutes longer, until a knife pierces the spear easily. Makes 4 servings.

Hot Asparagus Cheese Fingers

You may have seen or tried these made the old-fashioned way, with canned asparagus. These are so much tastier, and not much more work. Definitely a good choice for a party, but just as good for lunch.

12 thin asparagus spears, trimmed
12 slices white bread
½ pound Swiss cheese
2 tablespoons butter, softened
¼ to ½ cup Dijon mustard
4 tablespoons butter, melted

Preheat the oven to 450 degrees. Grease a baking sheet.

Combine the asparagus and 2 tablespoons water in a microwaveable casserole. Cover and microwave for 2 to 4 minutes just until tender; drain. Transfer the asparagus to a bowl of ice water. Pat the asparagus dry.

Cut the crusts from the bread. Roll the bread slices with a rolling pin to ¼ inch thickness. Combine the Dijon and butter and spread the mixture on one side of the bread.

Slice the cheese into pieces about ¼ inch wide and the length of the bread. Arrange an asparagus spear and a cheese slice on one end of each bread slice. Roll to enclose. Place seam side down on a baking sheet. Brush with melted butter. Bake for 10 minutes until browned and bubbly. Serve hot.
Makes 12 rolls.

Crisp Sesame Ginger Asparagus

1 pound asparagus spears, trimmed
Sesame Ginger Vinaigrette
1 tablespoon sesame seeds
1 teaspoon grated fresh ginger
1 garlic clove
1 tablespoon sugar
2 teaspoons soy sauce
2 tablespoons rice vinegar
2 tablespoons orange juice
1 tablespoon vegetable oil
1/3 teaspoon red pepper flakes
3 tablespoons sesame oil

Steam the asparagus in a small amount of boiling salted water for 3 minutes until tender-crisp; drain. Pat dry and arrange on a serving platter or bowl.

Toast the sesame seeds in a small skillet, stirring frequently, until golden. Combine the sesame seeds and remaining ingredients in a blender and blend until thoroughly combined. Pour some of the dressing over the asparagus spears. Can be chilled in the refrigerator for a day. The dressing keeps for up to a month. Makes 4 servings.

Taking the Harvest to the Table

Beans (snap)

When to harvest

Pick snap beans while beans inside the pods are immature. Old pods are tough and lose their taste, and some will develop strings along their seams.

Pick all mature pods even if you are not able to eat them. If the beans are left on the vine, the plant will stop producing. Bush beans will continue to produce for about three weeks if kept picked. Pole beans can yield all season long.

Signs that it is ready

Pods are a useful size and smooth along their length, without the visible bumps of growing beans, or with very small bumps.

When is it too late?

If pods become overripe and tough because you could not get to them, allow them to dry on the vine and harvest the beans inside for dried beans.

How to harvest

It's better to cut the stem rather than try to pull off the beans by breaking the stem.

Expected yield

Bush beans will produce a big handful per plant for the first harvests, then about half that for the second setting of fruit. Pole beans produce just a few at a time but once started, continually produce through the entire season.

TIPS

- *Storage*
  Store freshly picked snap beans in the refrigerator in plastic bags. They will stay relatively fresh for a week or so. Snap bean pods will keep in the freezer up to 12 months. They can also be canned in a pressure steamer or pickled.

- *Eat / Don't Eat*
  Both pods and the beans inside are edible.

- *Companion Planting*
  Native Americans planted beans with corn and squash. They were called the Three Sisters because they grow well together and support each other. The beans grow up the corn stalks (the first no-work, no-pole method) and the large prickly squash leaves and stems prevented the racoons from stealing the corn.

KID'S CORNER

We all know that vegetables start to deteriorate and lose vitamins and minerals the minute they are harvested or cut from the vine. It is true that with refrigeration and packaging, they can last for a long time, but there's nothing like fresh. Try this taste test with beans. Harvest three green beans of about the same size. Eat one right on the spot in the garden. Next, leave one on the kitchen counter for an hour before eating. Put the third one in the refrigerator for a day before eating. Make out a little questionnaire to compare tastes, textures, and enjoyment of the three beans. Try this taste test on your parents and record their answers, too.

Mel says…

One of the many advantages of Square Foot Gardening is that you're not overwhelmed with too much of one vegetable ripening at once. Early in the season, you'll probably have just a few beans ripe at once. Go ahead and pick them when they're small and use them raw in salad, or combine them with a few other vegetables in a stir-fry.

Taking the Harvest to the Table

Beans (dried)

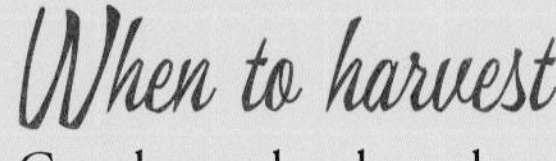

When to harvest

Cut the pods when they are dry and the beans rattle inside.

When is it too late?

It's best to harvest dry beans before the pods split and the beans fall to the ground.

How to harvest

With large pole bean plants, pick the pods off. Bush or other smaller plants should be cut down at soil level when pods turn yellow. Hang the plants in a warm, dry place until the seeds rattle in the pods. They can be hung outside, or in a garage, porch, or attic. You can hang the plants themselves or put them into burlap or mesh bags. Beans are fully dry when they can't be dented by biting into them.

Threshing removes the dried beans from the pods. Put the plants, pods and all, in a big burlap or cloth bag. Shake or beat the bag to loosen the beans from the pods. Or let children jump up and down on the bag. Then cut off a small corner of the bag and let the beans drop out, leaving the plants and pods inside.

TIPS

■ *Storage*

Store well-dried beans in airtight jars. Put a tablespoon of powdered milk in a folded paper towel inside each jar of dried beans to absorb any moisture left in the beans while they're in storage. Dry beans will keep well in a cool, dry, dark spot.

■ *Eat / Don't Eat*

Beans are edible, but not pods.

Make-Your-Own Salade Niçoise with Basil Vinaigrette

A Niçoise "salad bar" lets each person select only favorite ingredients, or pile up some of everything for an authentic Niçoise.

Basil Vinaigrette

¾ cup olive oil or vegetable oil
¼ cup red wine vinegar
½ teaspoon salt
Freshly ground black pepper to taste
1 green onion
6 large parsley leaves
6 basil leaves, optional

Salad Bar

4 to 6 fist-size red potatoes, cut into ¼-inch slices
1½ pounds green beans, trimmed, cut into 1½-inch lengths
6 cups chopped romaine lettuce
2 large tomatoes, cut into wedges
3 hard-boiled eggs, cut into quarters
½ cup Niçoise olives
2 or 3 (5-ounce) cans oil-pack tuna, drained, finely flaked

For the dressing, combine the oil, vinegar, salt, pepper, green onion, parsley and basil in a blender or food processor. Process until herbs are puréed and mixture is emulsified.

For the salad bar, cook the potatoes and green beans either separately or together in boiling salted water for 5 minutes (for the beans) to 8 minutes (for the potatoes) until tender; drain. Combine the warm potatoes and beans separately with a little of the dressing.

Arrange the lettuce, tomatoes, eggs, olives, tuna, potatoes and beans in bowls. Set the dressing at the end of the "salad bar." Makes 6 to 8 side dish servings or 4 main dish servings.

Salade Niçoise with Basil Vinaigrette

Stir-Fried Beef & Green Beans

When your harvest is just a handful of green beans, toss them into a stir-fry.

- 2 cups peanut or canola oil
- 4 to 8 ounces (about 2 handfuls) green beans, trimmed
- 8 ounces flank steak, cut across the grain into thin slices
- 2 teaspoons soy sauce
- 2 teaspoons dry sherry or rice wine
- ½ teaspoon grated fresh ginger
- 2 teaspoons cornstarch
- 3 tablespoons peanut or canola oil
- ½ cup sliced red bell pepper
- 2 teaspoons bean sauce
- ¼ cup beef broth
- Pinch of sugar
- 1 teaspoon dark sesame oil

Heat the oil to 360 degrees in a 2- or 3-quart saucepan. Add the green beans and deep fry for 1 minute; stay back, as they will spatter. Drain on paper towels.

Combine the steak, soy sauce, sherry, ginger and cornstarch in a bowl and mix well. Stir-fry in 1 tablespoon of the oil in a skillet or wok over high heat. Clean out the skillet.

Heat 2 tablespoons of oil in the skillet and add the bell pepper. Stir-fry for 1 minute. Add the bean sauce, broth and sugar and mix well. Add the beef and green beans. Stir-fry to coat with the mixture and heat through. Drizzle with sesame oil. Serve with rice or rice noodles. Makes 2 to 3 servings.

Roasted Green Beans

Choose young snap or bush beans for roasting – runner or pole beans are not juicy enough for roasting. Fresh rosemary leaves, if you have them, are a better choice than dried, because they stay tender when roasted.

- 1 pound tender young green beans, trimmed
- Salt and freshly ground black pepper to taste
- 2 garlic cloves, pressed or minced
- ½ teaspoon fresh rosemary leaves, or 1 teaspoon dried rosemary
- 2 tablespoons olive oil

Preheat the oven to 400 degrees. Combine the beans, salt, pepper, garlic, rosemary and olive oil in a plastic bag. Close the bag and shake to coat the beans with the other ingredients. Spread the beans on a roasting pan or baking sheet with a rim. Roast for 25 minutes, stirring the beans after 15 minutes. Makes 4 small servings.

Refrigerator-Pickled Beans

As beans ripen, you can add them to the jar after boiling them for a minute or two. The beans are good for snacking, or make a great swizzle stick in a Bloody Mary.

8 ounces (2 handfuls) green beans, stems cut off, beans trimmed to fit jars
¾ cup white wine vinegar
1 cup cider vinegar
½ cup water
2 teaspoons salt
1 tablespoon sugar
3 garlic cloves, sliced or smashed
1 tablespoon black peppercorns
2 teaspoons mustard seeds
2 teaspoons dill or fennel seeds
1 inch dried red pepper pod or ¼ teaspoon red pepper flakes
2 bay leaves

Simmer the beans in a large pan of water for 2 minutes until tender-crisp; drain. Chill the beans in ice water; drain well.

Combine the vinegars, water, salt, sugar, garlic, peppercorns, mustard seeds, dill seeds, pepper and bay leaves over high heat. Bring to a boil; cook for 1 minute to dissolve the sugar and salt.

Pack the beans and garlic into a clean, glass 1-pint jar (a tall one will hold long beans without trimming). Pour the vinegar mixture over the beans—they should be completely covered. Top with a lid. Chill in the refrigerator for 2 days. The beans will keep in the refrigerator for at least 4 weeks. Makes about 1 pint.

Roasted Green Bean & Potato Salad

For the best texture, serve the salad the day it is made.

2 pounds small red potatoes, cut into chunks
2 tablespoons vegetable oil
1 teaspoon coarse salt
Freshly ground black pepper
½ supersweet onion, thinly sliced
1 small shallot or large garlic clove
¼ cup white wine vinegar
½ cup olive oil
1 teaspoon fresh rosemary leaves
Coarse salt and freshly ground pepper to taste
1 pound green beans, trimmed, cut into 1-inch pieces

Preheat the oven to 400 degrees. Combine the potatoes, vegetable oil, salt and pepper in a bowl and mix well. Arrange the potatoes in a single layer in a roasting pan. Roast for 30 minutes, stirring occasionally, until they are tender and browned. Let cool slightly.

Combine the onion with ice water to cover in a bowl and let stand for 15 minutes while the potatoes roast; drain and pat the onion dry.

Purée the shallot, vinegar, olive oil, rosemary, salt and pepper in a blender or food processor. Combine the dressing with the warm potatoes in a large bowl.

Cook the green beans in boiling salted water for 5 minutes until tender-crisp; drain. Rinse them under cold running water. Pat the green beans dry. Add to the bowl with the potatoes. Add the onion and mix well. Makes 6 servings.

Pole Beans with Garlic & Sweet Onions

This recipe is ideal for romano beans, the long and flat variety, or any bean that's tender when young but grows tough as it matures.

1 pound pole beans, trimmed, cut into 1-inch pieces
2 garlic cloves, pressed or minced
½ cup chopped supersweet onion
1 tablespoon vegetable oil
2 cups water
Salt and pepper to taste
2 tablespoons brown sugar

Sauté the garlic and onion in vegetable oil in a Dutch oven or flameproof casserole dish for 5 minutes until tender. Add the beans, water, salt, pepper and brown sugar. Reduce the heat to simmer, cover and cook for 30 to 40 minutes until beans are tender but not mushy. Drain the beans. Add more salt and pepper before serving. Makes 4 to 6 servings.

Green Bean Munchers

Just like those battered, fried appetizers at restaurants, and sure to appeal to kids who don't especially enjoy green beans.

- 1 to 1½ cups buttermilk pancake mix
- ½ teaspoon ground coriander or seasoned salt
- 2 to 4 cups vegetable oil for frying
- 1 pound (about 4 handfuls) fresh green beans, trimmed, kept whole
- ½ cup freshly grated Parmesan cheese

Prepare the pancake mix according to the package directions, adding coriander. Heat at least 2 inches of oil in a heavy pot or deep fryer to 375 degrees. Using tongs or a slotted spoon, dip a few green beans into the batter, letting the excess drip back into the bowl. Carefully lower the beans, one or two at a time, into the hot oil. Break them up if they stick together.

Fry until golden brown. (Cook them a little longer rather than erring on the side of undercooking.) Remove from the oil and drain on paper towels. Sprinkle with the Parmesan cheese right away. Serve immediately, or keep hot briefly in a 250-degree oven. Makes 6 servings.

Crisp Green Beans with Blue Cheese & Walnuts

- 1 pound green beans
- ½ teaspoon Dijon mustard
- 1 teaspoon white wine vinegar
- 2 tablespoons olive oil
- Salt and freshly ground pepper to taste
- ⅔ cup walnuts or pecans, toasted and coarsely chopped
- 2 ounces blue cheese, crumbled

Cook the beans in boiling salted water to cover for 3 minutes, just until tender; drain. Rinse well with cold water. Drain and pat dry.

Whisk the mustard, vinegar, olive oil, salt and pepper in a large bowl. Add the beans and mix well. Top with the walnuts and blue cheese. Makes 4 servings.

Taking the Harvest to the Table

Broccoli

When to harvest

Pick the first head of broccoli from each plant when it is well formed. Each tiny green dot on the head is a flower bud; be sure to harvest before they begin to bloom. If you wait too long, you can still cook and eat stalks with flowers that have started to open, but the open buds turn brownish when cooked. Continue harvesting the much smaller, successive heads as they form on the plant.

Signs that it is ready

Broccoli is ready to pick when the first bunch at the center of the plant is about four inches in diameter. New, smaller heads will form on the lower stalk.

When is it too late?

The head will grow and grow, getting bigger and bigger, so it's hard to say, "OK, that's enough; you're dinner now." But if you wait too long, within days you will see tiny yellow color showing on the head; these are flowers going to seed and the plant will stop producing if it makes flowers. It will also lose its great fresh and unique taste and structure then.

How to harvest

Cut the stalk off the plant a few inches below the head with a sharp knife or large garden shears.

TIPS

■ *Storage*

Refrigerate loosely wrapped broccoli for up to two weeks. To freeze broccoli, first cut the heads into small chunks, then blanch for three minutes. Frozen broccoli will retain most of its flavor and color for six months. Broccoli can also be canned or pickled.

■ *Eat / Don't Eat*

The unopened flower buds (the head) and the stalks are edible.

■ *Companion Planting*

Plant broccoli near herbs such as dill, celery, chamomile, sage, peppermint, and rosemary, or with potatoes, beets, and onions. Do not plant with tomatoes, pole beans, or strawberries. Nasturtiums will attract aphids, which can help keep them off the broccoli.

■ *This 'n' That*

Studies suggest that broccoli can help lower high blood pressure.

KID'S CORNER

Do a blind taste test with a bite of broccoli from the grocery store, and one fresh from your garden. Wear a blindfold so you can't see the bites. Which broccoli has a crisper texture? Does one have a sweeter taste? A "greener" flavor? Which tastes more like "the outdoors"? Which would you rather eat? That information can help you decide how to prepare broccoli, and whether you want to include it in next year's garden.

PENNY PINCHER

Homegrown broccoli produces lots of leaves, which are edible but can be slightly bitter. Harvest them and use them together with chard, kale, arugula, and other cooked greens.

Mel says…

Growing your own broccoli organically eliminates many health concerns you might have about pesticides and insecticides in the food supply, and about contamination that may have occurred during shipment and handling.

Sesame & Orange-Scented Beef & Broccoli

For the sauce, combine the juice, broth, soy sauce, sesame oil and cornstarch in a bowl; set aside.

For the stir-fry: Combine the meat and the soy sauce in a bowl. Heat a large skillet over high heat. Add 1 tablespoon of the oil and heat until just smoking. Add the beef and stir-fry for 3 minutes until browned. Transfer to a bowl.

Sesame Orange Sauce

½ cup orange juice, preferably freshly squeezed
¼ cup chicken broth
¼ cup soy sauce
2 teaspoons dark sesame oil
2 teaspoons cornstarch

Stir-fry

1 pound flat-iron or flank steak, cut into thin strips
2 teaspoons soy sauce
3 tablespoons peanut or vegetable oil
3 cups broccoli florets and peeled, chopped stems
½ cup water
1 bell pepper or 2 sweet banana peppers, cored, seeded, cut into strips
3 garlic cloves, minced
1 tablespoon grated fresh ginger
1 tablespoon sesame seeds, toasted

Add 1 more tablespoon of oil to the pan. Heat until the oil shimmers. Add the broccoli and water. Cook, covered, for 2 minutes until the broccoli is bright green and tender-crisp. Add the pepper and cook for 3 minutes until tender.

Move the vegetables to one side of the skillet. Turn the heat to medium-low and add the last tablespoon of oil and the garlic and ginger. Cook gently for about 30 seconds until fragrant. Add the beef to the pan. Stir the sauce ingredients and pour over the beef and vegetables. Cook, stirring, for 1 to 2 minutes until the sauce thickens. Sprinkle with the sesame seeds. Makes 4 to 6 servings.

Sesame & Orange-Scented Beef & Broccoli

Creamy Chicken Broccoli Skillet

Use chicken breast, or leftover deboned chicken meat, in a skillet meal that will remind many people of mom's cooking.

- 2 (8-ounce) cans cream of chicken soup
- 1 cup sour cream
- ½ cup half-and-half or evaporated milk
- 1 cup milk
- 1 tablespoon garlic powder
- 1 tablespoon black pepper
- 1 teaspoon seasoned salt or herb seasoning mix
- 2 chicken breasts, cooked and diced
- 2 cups shredded white cheddar or other flavorful white cheese
- 2 cups chopped broccoli crowns and stems
- Hot cooked rice

Combine the soup, sour cream, half-and-half, milk, garlic powder, pepper and seasoned salt in a large saucepan or skillet and mix well. Heat the mixture over medium-low heat, stirring, until warm. Add the chicken and cook, stirring occasionally, until the mixture begins to bubble. Add the cheese and cook, stirring occasionally, until melted.

Steam or microsteam the broccoli for 3 to 5 minutes until it reaches your preferred tenderness; drain. Add to the chicken mixture in the skillet and mix well. Serve over hot cooked rice. Makes 4 to 6 servings.

Crisp Cool Broccoli Salad

- 3 tablespoons red wine vinegar
- ¼ cup sugar, or to taste
- ½ cup mayonnaise
- 6 slices bacon, chopped, cooked, drained
- 3 stalks young broccoli, cut into florets, stems peeled
- ½ cup minced celery
- ½ cup minced red onion
- ½ cup broken pecan pieces
- ½ cup craisins or golden raisins

Broccoli becomes a refreshing salad paired with bacon and the surprise sweetness of craisins.

Combine the vinegar and sugar in the bottom of a salad bowl and stir to dissolve the sugar. Whisk in the mayonnaise. Add the bacon, broccoli, celery and onion to the bowl and stir to coat with the mayonnaise mixture. Top with the pecans and craisins. Makes 6 servings.

Creamy Chicken Broccoli Skillet

Broccoli & Red Pepper Salad with Herb Cream

Salad

3 stalks broccoli
1 red bell pepper

Herb Cream

½ cup olive oil
½ cup sour cream
2 teaspoons Dijon mustard
½ cup tarragon or basil leaves
2 tablespoons tarragon or basil vinegar
Salt and freshly ground pepper to taste

Cut the broccoli into bite-size pieces. Steam or boil in salted water for 3 minutes until tender. Rinse with cold water; drain thoroughly. Combine the broccoli and red pepper in a medium bowl.

Combine the olive oil, sour cream, mustard, tarragon, vinegar, salt and pepper in a blender or food processor. Process until tarragon is well-chopped. Pour the herb cream over the broccoli and pepper. Toss to coat. Makes 6 servings.

Broccoli in Garlic Brown Butter

Classic recipes like this one depend on a few simple, high-quality ingredients treated with a light hand.

3 stalks broccoli, cut into bite-size pieces
¼ cup vegetable or olive oil
6 garlic cloves
4 tablespoons butter
A few drops of lemon juice

Steam or microsteam the broccoli for 3 to 5 minutes until tender; drain. Rinse with cold water; drain well. Heat the olive oil in a medium skillet over low heat until hot. Add the garlic and let it "sweat" for 5 minutes until the garlic is tender but not browned. Remove from the heat.

In another skillet or small saucepan, heat the butter over medium-low heat until it foams and begins to brown. Watch carefully, as it goes from brown to burned quickly. When the butter is brown, remove it from the heat immediately. Pour the browned butter into the skillet. Add the lemon juice and mix well. Add the broccoli to the skillet and toss to coat. Makes 4 servings.

Italian Chopped Vegetable Salad for a Crowd

A great solution if your garden runneth over! Taste the broccoli before making the salad—if it's tender and delicate tasting, use it raw. Otherwise, steam or boil it for 2 minutes, then rinse it with cold water.

- 6 ounces balsamic vinaigrette or good-quality Italian salad dressing
- 1 envelope Italian salad dressing mix
- 12 green onions, sliced
- ½ cup chopped fresh parsley or basil
- 1 (9-ounce) jar chopped green olives, drained
- 3 broccoli stalks, cut into bite-size pieces
- 1 head cauliflower, cut into florets
- 1 cup chopped sweet pepper, any color
- 2 cups diced celery or ½ cup minced lovage stems
- 2 medium zucchini, chopped
- 1 medium cucumber, diced

Combine the dressing, dressing mix, green onions, parsley and olives in the bottom of a large salad bowl and mix well. (You may need to use two bowls.) Add the broccoli, cauliflower, bell pepper, celery, zucchini and cucumber and mix well. Chill, covered, for 4 hours. Makes 20 servings.

Horseradish Broccoli Sandwich Topper

A great use for broccoli stems that adds flavor and nutrition to sandwiches. Imagine what this mixture can do for a turkey sandwich!

- 2 to 3 broccoli stems
- ⅓ cup sour cream
- 2 tablespoons spicy brown mustard
- 1 teaspoon prepared horseradish
- 2 tablespoons snipped fresh chives
- ½ teaspoon sugar
- Salt to taste

Peel the broccoli stems. Grate them on a coarse grater or in a food processor. Combine the sour cream, mustard, horseradish, chives, sugar and salt in a bowl and mix well. Add the broccoli and mix well. Let stand 15 minutes for the flavors to blend. Use the mixture on sandwiches. Makes 1 to 1½ cups.

Taking the Harvest to the Table

Cabbage

When to harvest

Harvest cabbage when the head is completely formed but while still firm to the touch. You can pick the outer leaves of Chinese cabbage while the plant is growing, or leave the big outer leaves and cut the head when it is formed.

Signs that it is ready

Cabbage can be harvested any time after the head forms and feels firm when squeezed.

When is it too late?

Harvest before the heads crack or split open, as a seed stalk will rise from that split and the sweet cabbage flavor will become bitter.

How to harvest

GREEN CABBAGE: Pull the cabbage head from the soil, roots and all, to store outside or in a root cellar; cut the head at soil level to store in the refrigerator.

CHINESE CABBAGE: Pick outer leaves as the plant grows, or wait until the head forms. Cut the head off at the base with a sharp knife.

Expected yield

1 head per square foot

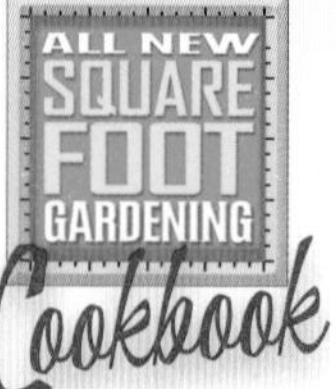

TIPS

KID'S CORNER

If you grow cabbage, it's likely you have cabbage worms. The big holes in the leaves are your clue. Use this as an opportunity to learn more about garden pests. Where do you find the worm? What color is it? Is there more than one? Ambitious entomologists can draw the bug and the munched cabbage leaves. Note how it eats. Does it eat from the outside edge around right to left or left to right? Does it eat from the center and right to left or left to right?

■ *Storage*

In cool weather, store green cabbage in a root cellar where the temperature stays above freezing but below 45 degrees. Hang them by their roots or wrap the heads in newspaper. Storing cabbage in the house can be odiferous as the cabbages mature. Cabbage can be refrigerated for about two weeks in a paper bag or a plastic bag with holes it in for air circulation. Chinese cabbage can be stored the same way for about a week. Cabbage can also be pickled as sauerkraut.

■ *Eat / Don't Eat*

Cabbage leaves and heads are edible but the outer big leaves may not be as tasty and tender.

■ *Companion Planting*

Plant cabbage near herbs such as dill, celery, chamomile, sage, peppermint, and rosemary, or with potatoes, beets, and onions. Do not plant with tomatoes, pole beans, or strawberries. Nasturtium will attract aphids and can help keep them off the cabbage.

■ *This 'n' That*

Cabbage is one of the oldest known vegetables, grown in both the East and the West.

Mel says...

Why do we plant flowers in our Square Foot gardens? Because they're pretty, but also, flowers and herbs attract beneficial insects that prey on the creatures eating your Brassica *crops—cabbage, broccoli, and Brussels sprouts.*

Cabbage Rolls

There are so many versions of cabbage rolls—Hungarians add a sour cream and sauerkraut sauce that keeps the rolls from drying as they cook and creates a creamy, tomatoey sauce. The rolls freeze well after cooking, so it makes sense to prepare a big batch.

12 large cabbage leaves
1 onion, chopped
4 tablespoons butter
¼ cup chopped celery or parsley
1¼ pounds ground beef or pork
1 tablespoon paprika
1 teaspoon garlic powder
2 cups cooked rice
1 egg, optional
Salt and pepper to taste
Dried basil, thyme or rosemary to taste
1 (15-ounce) can sauerkraut, drained, rinsed
2 (8-ounce) cans tomato sauce
1 cup sour cream

Cut off the cabbage leaves near the core. Boil them in a large pot of water for 3 to 4 minutes until they are softened; drain. Lay them flat and trim off some of the hard, thick rib. Cut a "V" at the base of the rib to simplify rolling.

Sauté the onion in the butter in a large skillet over medium-high heat for 8 minutes until tender. Add the celery and cook for 2 minutes. Add the meat and cook until browned and crumbly. Drain and discard most of the fat in the skillet. Add the paprika and garlic powder and cook, stirring, for 2 minutes.

Preheat the oven to 350 degrees. Combine the meat, rice, egg, salt and herbs in a bowl and mix well. Spoon a tablespoon or two of filling into each roll. Roll to enclose the filling, tucking in the sides to make a secure package. Arrange the rolls in a baking dish or a slow cooker that holds them snugly. (Two or three layers is fine, and prevents drying out.) Spread the sauerkraut over the rolls, then pour the tomato sauce over them. Cover and bake for 45 minutes, or cook in a slow cooker on low for 6 to 8 hours.

Stir the sour cream and pour over the rolls. Bake 5 to 10 minutes longer (but don't let the sauce boil) or 20 minutes in the slow cooker on high. Serve with or without the sour cream sauce. Makes 12 rolls.

Cabbage Rolls

Fish Tacos & Cucumber Cilantro Slaw

Healthful, full of exciting flavors, and so easy for a weeknight supper.

4 frozen battered fish fillets
4 (8-inch) flour tortillas
1 tablespoon mayonnaise
1 tablespoon fresh lime juice
½ teaspoon cumin seed or ¼ teaspoon ground cumin
Salt and pepper to taste
2 cups shredded or chopped green cabbage
2 tablespoons chopped fresh cilantro, or to taste
1 green onion, sliced or minced
½ cup chopped fresh cucumber, optional
1 teaspoon chopped jalapeño or serrano chili, or to taste

Bake the fish fillets according to the package directions.

Wrap the tortillas in aluminum foil and place them in the oven to heat. Or heat them at the last minute in a microwave in plastic wrap.

Combine the mayonnaise, lime juice, cumin, salt and pepper in a medium bowl. Add the cabbage, cilantro, green onion, cucumber and jalapeño, and mix well.

Cut each hot fish fillet into 6-8 pieces, then pile into a hot tortilla with lots of slaw. Makes 4 servings.

Blue Cheese Slaw

Lemon and blue cheese plus crunchy vegetables create a salad nice enough for company but simple enough for weeknights.

Juice of 2 lemons (about ¼ cup)
2 teaspoons Dijon mustard
½ cup olive oil
Salt and freshly ground pepper to taste
¼ cup crumbled blue cheese
2 cups shredded cabbage
1 large or 2 small sweet peppers, deseeded, chopped
1 cup sliced fresh snow peas or sugar snaps
1 small carrot, shredded

Combine the juice, mustard, oil, salt, pepper and blue cheese in a salad bowl with a fork or whisk until blended. Add the cabbage, bell pepper, snow peas and carrot and mix well to coat with the dressing. Serve chilled or at room temperature. Makes 4 servings.

Fish Tacos & Cucumber Cilantro Slaw

Noodles & Browned Cabbage

This Hungarian supper gets its flavor depth from the skillet-browned cabbage, which gets extra dimensions of taste when its sugars caramelize in the heat.

- 1 stick (½ cup) butter
- 1 large onion, sliced
- 6 cups sliced cabbage
- 1 teaspoon salt
- Freshly ground pepper to taste
- 8 to 16 ounces egg noodles
- 1 cup sour cream, optional

Sauté the onion and cabbage in the butter in a Dutch oven or small soup pot for 10 to 15 minutes until tender. Add salt and pepper. Reduce the heat to low, cover, and cook for 15 minutes.

Cook the noodles according to package directions; drain. Add to the cabbage mixture and mix well. Add salt if needed. Serve the sour cream on the side for topping. Makes 4 servings.

Cabbage Baked with Feta

This hearty dish is satisfying enough for a meatless entrée. Just add bread and fruit.

- 8 to 10 cups sliced green cabbage
- 2 tablespoons butter
- 2 tablespoons vegetable oil
- ¼ cup sour cream or plain whole milk yogurt
- 2 eggs
- 3 tablespoons fresh or dried dill
- Salt and freshly ground pepper to taste
- ½ cup bread crumbs
- 1 cup crumbled feta cheese
- 4 tablespoons butter
- 1 teaspoon sweet or smoked paprika

Cook the cabbage in boiling salted water for 2 minutes; drain very well. Sauté the cabbage in the butter and oil in a large skillet over medium heat for 15 minutes until browned.

Preheat the oven to 375 degrees. Beat the sour cream and eggs in a small bowl. Add the cabbage, dill, salt and pepper and mix well. Spoon the mixture into a greased baking dish.

Combine the bread crumbs and feta cheese in a small bowl. Spread over the cabbage mixture. Drizzle with the melted butter and dust with the paprika. Bake for 15 to 20 minutes or until the bread crumbs are crisp and browned. Makes 4 servings.

Two-Cheese Cabbage & Ham Salad

Use the optional romaine lettuce to stretch this cabbage, cheese and ham salad.

Lemon Blue Cheese Vinaigrette

¼ cup red wine vinegar
1 teaspoon salt
1 garlic clove, minced
2 teaspoons Dijon mustard
¾ cup olive oil
1/3 cup blue cheese, crumbled

Salad

4 to 6 cups shredded cabbage
½ pound baked ham, chopped
8 ounces Swiss cheese, sliced into matchsticks
¼ cup chopped fresh fennel leaf or parsley
4 cups torn romaine lettuce, optional

For the dressing, combine the vinegar and salt in a large salad bowl and mix well. Add the mustard, olive oil, garlic and blue cheese and mix well. Add the cabbage, ham, cheese and fennel and mix well. May be refrigerated for up to 6 hours. Serve on a bed of romaine lettuce. Makes 4 servings.

Cumin Cabbage & Rice

Cabbage and rice make a simple meatless meal, a base for spiced baked chicken, or a memorable side dish.

2 medium onions, sliced
2 tablespoons vegetable oil
4 garlic cloves, sliced
8 cups sliced green cabbage
1 teaspoon salt
1 teaspoon freshly ground pepper
½ teaspoon ground turmeric
2 teaspoons ground cumin
2 cups long grain rice, white or brown
4 cups vegetable broth or chicken broth

Sauté the onions in the oil in a large pan over medium heat for 5 to 7 minutes, stirring occasionally, until tender. Reduce the heat to low. Add the garlic, cabbage and salt and mix well. Cook, covered, for 10 minutes, stirring occasionally, until the cabbage is wilted.

Add the pepper, turmeric, cumin and rice and sauté for 2 to 3 minutes until the rice is transparent. Add the broth and mix well. Bring to a boil, cover, and cook white rice for 20 minutes, brown rice for 45 minutes. Makes 6 to 8 servings.

Taking the Harvest to the Table

Carrots

When to harvest

Carrots can be harvested any time between bite-size and maximum size, depending on the variety.

Signs that it is ready

A carrot can be pulled any time after it reaches a usable size.

When is it too late?

Carrots left in the ground too long develop a woody texture and lose their flavor. Check the seed packet and harvest carrots before they reach their maximum size.

How to harvest

For a Square Foot garden with a loose, friable soil mix, just grab the largest tops and pull that carrot out of the ground, swish it around in your bucket of sun-warmed water, and it is ready to eat right in the garden. Or you can cut off the tops and take it into the kitchen for same-day use.

Expected yield

Each square foot will produce sixteen carrots, or two large bunches of carrots.

TIPS

KID'S CORNER

Make a study to see what animals will eat carrots. One way is to visit a zoo to see what's in the animals' plates or eating trays. You could also ask the zookeeper. Then try your own pets. Dog? Cat? Snake, mouse, or hamster? Birds? Go to a farm and try goats, cows, and horses. Always ask permission first. As a special game, get others to guess ahead and make up a chart to record the results.

Storage

Carrots can over-winter in the ground in mild climates. Where the soil freezes, you can cover that garden area with a bale of hay and just roll it off anytime you want to harvest a few, then roll it back to protect the rest. Another way is to harvest them all and store in a root cellar in a barrel of moist sand. Don't let them touch each other. Store them away from apples so they don't get bitter. Washed, leafless carrots can be refrigerated for two to four weeks. Carrots can also be canned or frozen.

Eat / Don't Eat

Carrot roots are edible. Cut leaves off the carrot roots right away after harvesting. The leaves continue growing, taking moisture and nourishment from the roots, leaving them limp, wrinkled, and tasteless. Toss carrot tops in the compost bin.

Companion Planting

Plant carrots with onions or leeks. Rosemary, wormwood, and sage can repel the carrot fly.

This 'n' That

Carrots come in a large variety of shapes, sizes, and colors, from extra long to the size and shape of a ping pong ball, and from white to purple with yellow inside.

Mel says...

Rather than buying carrots in a plastic bag which will be sent to the landfill, you can walk to your garden and pull carrots. There's no packaging or other waste to be disposed of whatsoever. The carrot tops go into the compost pile. No travel to the store, no packaging to discard—think of the impact this could have on the environment if more people grew more of their own food.

Quick Balsamic Carrots

6 medium carrots, peeled, cut into rounds, or 12 to 15 baby or very young carrots
1 tablespoon butter
Salt to taste
1 tablespoon butter
2 tablespoons brown sugar, or to taste
1 teaspoon fine-quality balsamic vinegar

Combine the carrots with the butter and ¼ cup water in a small saucepan. Bring to a simmer over low heat. Simmer for 10 to 15 minutes until tender but not mushy; drain if needed.

Combine the butter, brown sugar and balsamic vinegar in a saucepan over low hêat. Cook, stirring, until sugar dissolves. Add the carrots and mix well. Makes 4 servings.

Carrot Timbale with Herb Crisp

Fresh thyme has a sweet, perfumey flavor—add it to your Square Foot garden.

1 pound carrots, peeled, cut into chunks
5 garlic cloves, sliced
1 teaspoon sugar
1 cup cream
1 cup milk
4 eggs, beaten
Salt and freshly ground pepper to taste
2 tablespoons Parmesan cheese
⅓ to ½ cup coarse bread crumbs
1 teaspoon fresh or dried thyme
2 tablespoons butter, melted

Bring the carrots, garlic and sugar to a boil in water to cover; simmer for 15 minutes until the carrots are very tender. Drain. Purée the carrots in a food processor. Add the milk and cream and blend thoroughly. Add the eggs, 2 tablespoons of Parmesan and salt and pepper; mix well.

Preheat the oven to 350 degrees. Grease a small casserole dish (about 1 quart). Sprinkle enough Parmesan cheese into the dish to cover the bottom and sides. Pour in the carrot mixture. Set the dish in a roasting pan and pour in hot water to reach 1 inch up the sides. Bake for 40 minutes.

Combine the butter, thyme and bread crumbs in a small bowl and mix well. Spread the mixture on a baking sheet and bake until crisp, watching closely. Serve each portion of carrot timbale sprinkled with a spoonful of herb crumbs. Makes 4 servings.

Quick Balsamic Carrots

Crunchy Carrot Slaw

Toasting the noodles yields a deeper flavor than the usual ramen noodle slaw. Tender baby spinach adds a buttery texture.

Rice Vinaigrette

1/3 cup rice vinegar or 1/4 cup cider vinegar
3/4 cup vegetable oil
1/4 cup sugar
2 teaspoons salt
1 teaspoon freshly ground black pepper

Slaw

2/3 cup sliced almonds or sunflower seeds
2 tablespoons sesame seeds
2 (3-ounce) packages ramen noodles
1 head cabbage, chopped
3 large or 6 small carrots, shredded
8 green onions, sliced
1 (10-ounce) package fresh baby spinach, optional

For the dressing, combine the vinegar, oil, sugar, salt and pepper in a bowl with a fork, or in a jar with a tight-fitting lid. Whisk or shake to combine.

Toast the almonds in a skillet over medium heat for 5 to 6 minutes. Add the sesame seeds and toast for 2 minutes longer. Remove and cool. Break up the noodles in the package; discard flavor packets. Toast the noodles in a skillet over medium heat for 5 to 6 minutes until lightly toasted in places. Combine the cabbage, carrots, green onions, spinach, almonds, sesame seeds and noodles in the bowl with the vinaigrette. Toss to combine with dressing up to 1½ hours before serving. Makes 8 to 10 servings.

Savory Carrot Olive Sandwich Spread

3 large carrots, grated
2/3 cup pecans or walnuts, minced or ground
1 garlic clove, minced
4 pimento-stuffed green olives, minced
2 teaspoons chopped fresh basil
Mayonnaise and/or softened cream cheese

Combine the carrots, pecans, garlic, green olives and basil with enough cream cheese and mayonnaise to hold the mixture together. Makes enough for 4 sandwiches.

Crunchy Carrot Slaw

Thai Roasted Vegetables

Vegetables

2 large or 6 small carrots, cut into chunks
1 medium potato, peeled, cut into chunks
1 medium sweet potato, peeled, cut into chunks
1 zucchini, cut into chunks
3 garlic cloves, sliced
1 small onion or shallot, sliced, optional
Vegetable oil

Peanut Coconut Sauce

3 tablespoons peanut butter
1 cup coconut milk
1 tablespoon fresh lime juice
1 tablespoon soy sauce, or to taste
Pinch of red pepper flakes
2 tablespoons water, if needed for thinning
Chopped mint and basil

Hot cooked rice

Preheat the oven to 400 degrees. Combine the carrots, potato, sweet potato, zucchini, garlic, onion and oil in a plastic bag and turn to coat the vegetables. Roast for 25 minutes, stirring twice.

Combine the peanut butter, coconut milk, lime juice, soy sauce and pepper flakes in a small saucepan. Cook, whisking, until warm and well-blended. Remove from the heat and pour over the roasted vegetables. Sprinkle with chopped mint and basil. Serve over hot cooked rice. Makes 4 servings.

Wintry Carrots Baked in Cream

Something extraordinary happens when carrots are baked a long time in cream—they become caramelized and buttery. If you're already baking something in the oven, just bake the carrots alongside at whatever that temperature may be.

1½ pounds carrots, grated
2 tablespoons butter
Salt and freshly ground pepper to taste
⅔ teaspoon freshly grated nutmeg
¾ cup heavy whipping cream

Preheat the oven to 400 degrees. Sauté the carrots in the butter in an ovenpoof skillet or casserole dish over medium-low heat for 2 to 3 minutes. Salt lightly and cook, stirring occasionally, for 5 minutes until the color changes. Add a little pepper, the nutmeg and the cream and mix well. Bring to a boil. Cover the skillet and place it in the oven. Bake for 30 to 40 minutes until the cream is absorbed and the carrots are browned at the pan's edges. Don't worry about overcooking—the carrots actually get better as they cook. Makes 4 servings.

Spiced Carrot Relish or Salad

Homegrown carrots sometimes have a sharper flavor than commercially grown varieties. Use them in this spiced concoction that's somewhere between a salad and a relish. For a mixture that's more like a salad, double the amount of carrots and cut them into matchsticks.

- ¼ teaspoon coriander seeds
- ¼ teaspoon fennel seeds
- ¼ teaspoon cardamom seeds
- ¼ teaspoon mustard seeds
- 1 garlic clove
- ½ teaspoon salt
- 1 teaspoon white wine vinegar
- 1 tablespoon lemon juice
- ¼ cup olive oil
- Freshly ground pepper to taste
- 1 pound carrots, shredded or cut into matchsticks
- 3 tablespoons sliced green onions

Grind the coriander, fennel, cardamom and mustard seeds in a grinder or mortar and pestle. Place the garlic on a cutting board and sprinkle it with the salt. Mince very fine—the garlic and salt should almost form a paste. Combine the spices and garlic mixture in a large bowl. Add the vinegar and lemon juice and mix well. Stir in the olive oil and pepper. Add the carrots and mix well. Sprinkle with green onions. Serve with meats, fish, poultry, cheeses and eggs. Keeps in the refrigerator for up to 2 weeks. Makes 4 small servings.

Sweet Peanut Carrot Spread

- ¼ cup crunchy peanut butter
- 1 to 2 tablespoons orange marmalade
- 1 large or 3 small carrots, shredded or grated
- 2 tablespoons raisins

Combine all of the ingredients in a small bowl and mix well. Use the mixture to fill sandwiches or spread it on crackers. Makes enough for 4 sandwiches.

Taking the Harvest to the Table

Cucumbers

When to harvest

Harvest cucumbers continuously or plant will stop making them.

Signs that it is ready

A cucumber is at its best when it is dark green, firm, and of moderate size. Harvest pickling-type cucumbers when they are three inches long. Pick slicing cucumbers when they are five to eight inches long.

When is it too late?

If you let just one fruit get overripe and begin turning yellow and tough, the plant will stop producing more fruit. Continuous picking actually increases a vine's production.

How to harvest

Cut or clip the cucumber from the plant with a knife or scissors, rather than twisting or pulling it off. Leave some of the stem on when you clip them, and use two hands so as not to break the fragile vines.

Expected yield

Generally, vining varieties will produce about fifteen cucumbers per plant and bush varieties will produce about ten per plant.

TIPS

KID'S CORNER

Here's an easy and entertaining garden project. You'll need a glass bottle. Find a cucumber that has flowered, been pollinated, and formed a tiny little cucumber. Slip the bottle over the cucumber and leave it for several days. Pretty soon it will be too large to slip the bottle off. The cucumber will continue growing—let it get as large as you like. When you're ready to harvest it, just cut off the stem. Then be ready to show off your amazing achievement! Don't try to break the glass bottle and eat the cucumber.

■ *Storage*

Cucumbers keep best in a cool, moist environment. Refrigerate them in plastic bags. They will keep for about a week, but they can lose their crispiness after five days. Whole cucumbers do not freeze well; they turn mushy when thawed. However, you can peel them, cut them up, and then freeze them. You can also grate or puree chunks of cucumbers and freeze the puree. Or, try baking fresh cucumber slices at 450° for 30 minutes before freezing them.

■ *Eat / Don't Eat*

The whole fruit is edible. Some people prefer to pare the skin while others like the look and taste of slices with skin. Tough skins should be peeled, and tender skins can be peeled in alternating strips down the length so slices will have alternate skin and flesh showing.

■ *Companion Planting*

Cucumbers grow well with beans, peas, radishes, and sunflowers. They seem to dislike potatoes and aromatic herbs.

■ *This 'n' That*

Cucumbers are said to help with high blood pressure.

Mel says...

There are types of cucumbers that are good for pickling and types that are good for eating fresh. Cucumber connoisseurs agree that pickling cucumbers taste good when chopped for salads, but that "slicing" cucumbers don't pickle very well. If you're looking for the most efficient garden plant, select a cucumber type whose label says that it is good for both pickling as well as eating fresh.

Creamy Cucumber & Radish Salad

A light, cool salad for hot days.

½ cup sour cream or plain yogurt
1 garlic clove, minced
1 teaspoon herb vinegar or white wine vinegar
Salt and freshly ground pepper to taste
1 large cucumber, sliced
1 bunch radishes (about 10), trimmed, sliced
2 tablespoons minced basil, dill or parsley

Combine the sour cream, garlic, vinegar, salt and pepper in a medium bowl. Arrange the cucumber and radishes on a platter or in a bowl.
Top with the sour cream mixture. Sprinkle with basil. Serve right away. Makes 4 servings.

Cucumber Sauce

This versatile sauce can take on different flavors. For an Indian raita, add a hot green chile and chopped mint. Turn it into Greek tzatziki by using yogurt, garlic and dill. For a sauce for cooked salmon, use sour cream, chives and a few capers.

1 large cucumber, peeled, seeds cut out if large, sliced
1 cup sour cream or plain yogurt
1 tablespoon lemon juice
1 teaspoon sliced green onion or chives
½ teaspoon salt

Combine the cucumber, yogurt, lemon juice, green onion and salt in a blender. Process in pulses until the cucumber and onion are finely chopped but not puréed. Makes 1½ cups.

Creamy Cucumber & Radish Salad

Cucumber Sandwiches

A classic for English tea, and a tempting lunch on a hot day. If you've made Green Goddess Dressing, page 80, you can use it to thin the cream cheese.

1 loaf sandwich bread
1 (8-ounce) package cream cheese, softened
3 tablespoons dry garlic-herb dressing mix
Milk for thinning, if needed
1 large cucumber, peeled, thinly sliced

Cut the crusts off the bread. Combine the cream cheese and dressing mix in a small bowl. Thin with a little milk to make a spreading consistency. Spread half of the mixture on half the bread slices. Top with cucumbers. Spread the remaining cream cheese mixture on the remaining bread. Top the sandwiches. Cut into fingers or triangles.

If you prefer, serve the sandwiches open-face, topped with a sprig of dill or a little paprika.

To keep cucumber sandwiches soft, dampen a paper towel then wring out all the water. Cover the sandwiches with the towel. Makes 16 to 18 servings.

Blue Moons

Blue Moons make a good appetizer, or a nice "finger salad."

3 ounces cream cheese, softened
3 ounces blue cheese or goat cheese, softened
Several drops of lemon juice
Salt to taste, optional
2 to 3 medium cucumbers, washed, cut into ¼-inch slices
Minced chives or dill for topping

Combine the cream cheese and blue cheese in a small bowl. Add the lemon juice and mix well. Taste the mixture and add salt if needed.

Arrange the cucumbers on a plate or platter. Spoon about ½ teaspoon of the mixture on each cucumber round. Top with a sprinkling of chives or dill. Makes 40 pieces.

Cucumber Sandwiches

Asian Cucumber Salad

Good for potluck, as it's tasty—and safe—at room temperature.

2 tablespoons rice wine vinegar
1 tablespoon soy sauce
1 teaspoon sugar
1 tablespoon sesame oil
1 tablespoon vegetable oil
Pinch of red pepper flakes
Salt to taste
3 large cucumbers, peeled and seeded
3 green onions, sliced
¼ cup chopped unsalted roasted peanuts

Combine the vinegar, soy sauce, sugar, oils, pepper flakes and salt in a medium bowl; stir until the sugar dissolves. Add the cucumbers and green onions and mix well. Let marinate for 1 hour either at room temperature or in the refrigerator. Sprinkle with peanuts to serve. Makes 4 to 6 servings.

Tuna & Cucumber Pasta Salad

Light and easy to make without much cooking.

Dressing

½ cup low-fat mayonnaise
½ cup low-fat sour cream
1 tablespoon lemon juice
2 tablespoons chopped fresh dill, or 1 tablespoon dried
Salt and freshly ground pepper to taste

Salad

1 pound shell or other small pasta shape
4 green onions, sliced
1 or 2 (5-ounce) cans albacore tuna in oil, or 8 ounces cured or smoked salmon
1 to 2 large cucumbers, peeled, deseeded if desired, chopped

For the dressing, combine the mayonnaise, sour cream, lemon juice, dill, salt and pepper in a large bowl and mix well.

Cook the pasta according to package directions. Drain and rinse with cold water. Drain again. Add to the dressing in the bowl. Drain and flake the tuna into the bowl. Mix to coat the ingredients with the dressing. Chill until ready to serve. Add the cucumbers and mix well. Serve within a few hours. Makes 10 servings.

Bread & Butter Refrigerator Pickles

Forget about the old way of pickling mountains of cucumbers. With a Square Foot garden, properly planted, you get a few cucumbers at a time, and this refrigerated method yields just a few jars of crisp, fresher-tasting pickles. ***Please note*** *that the pickling formula should only be used for pickles that will be stored in the refrigerator—the pickling solution isn't acidic enough for traditional water-bath process pickles.*

4 cucumbers, sliced
1 onion, sliced
1 tablespoon kosher or other non-iodized salt
Ice
1½ cups sugar
2 cups water
2 cups white vinegar
1 tablespoon mustard seeds
1 teaspoon celery seeds
½ teaspoon turmeric

Combine sliced cucumbers and onion and salt in a large bowl or other container. Cover generously with ice. Cover with a clean kitchen towel or plastic wrap and let stand 4 hours; drain, discarding any ice. Rinse the cucumbers and onions and drain well.

Combine sugar, water, vinegar, mustard seeds, celery seeds and turmeric in a large saucepan. Bring to a boil. Add the cucumbers and onions; return to a boil.

Spoon the cucumbers and onions into clean canning jars. Pour in enough of the liquid to cover. Top with a lid. Let cool to room temperature, then refrigerate. Let the pickles "pickle" for a few days. Store for up to a month in the refrigerator. Makes 4 to 5 pints.

Cucumber Ginger Limeade

It's easy to double and triple the recipe for this refreshing and surprising drink. It makes a wonderful ice pop, too, if you increase the sweetener a little.

1½ cups chopped, seeded, peeled cucumbers
⅓ cup frozen limeade concentrate, thawed
1 teaspoon grated fresh ginger
1 cup cold club soda
Lime wedges and cucumber slices

Combine the chopped cucumber, limeade and ginger in a blender or food processor. Cover and process until cucumber is puréed. Taste for sweetening. Combine the cucumber mixture and club soda in a small pitcher. Serve garnished with lime wedges and cucumber slices. Makes 2 servings.

Taking the Harvest to the Table

Eggplant

When to harvest

You don't have to wait until eggplant is mature to pick it. It can be only a third of its mature size and still taste good. This is its saving grace, and yours, too, since you don't have to worry too much about when to pick. When the fruits reach full size, roughly what you'd find at a farm stand or market, pick while the skins are still shiny.

Signs that it is ready

Press your thumb into the fruit. If it springs back, it is ready. Eggplant does not have to be fully mature to harvest. It can be eaten any time after it reaches one third of its mature size—some seed packets will state this. If frost threatens and the fruits are still tiny, use them as baby eggplants in stir-fries.

When is it too late?

When eggplant skin gets dull or brown it will not taste as good as when the skin is shiny.

How to harvest

Cut or snip, don't twist the eggplant from the stem. Twisting may work, but it may damage the plant or the fruit.

Expected yield

Four to six eggplants per square foot.

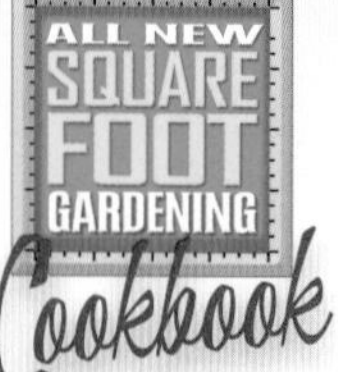

TIPS

■ *Storage*

Eggplant is perishable and becomes bitter with age. Refrigerate eggplant in a plastic bag for a day or two. If you plan to cook it the day you harvest it, leave it out at room temperature.

■ *Eat / Don't Eat*

Only the eggplant fruits are edible.

■ *Companion Planting*

Green beans can protect eggplant from the Colorado potato beetle. This beetle likes eggplant even better than potatoes, but is repelled by the beans.

■ *This 'n' That*

Eggplants come in many sizes and colors and are used in numerous cuisines throughout the world. Some are as small as grapes, and others are round and white like eggs.

KID'S CORNER

Grow something in your garden with, or for, your grandparents, no matter where they live. An eggplant is a good subject for sharing because it is easy to manage and has a limited harvest. Eggplants are simple to draw and are also photogenic. Share pictures or drawings of planting, and descriptions of the growth progress and harvest by email, regular mail, telephone, or in person. Better still, if grandparents live nearby or visit, involve them in the garden. This creates a wonderful bond, and is a subject that can be so easily enjoyed and discussed by different generations.

PENNY PINCHER

With Square Foot Gardening, you use just a pinch of seeds, not the entire pack, so when you sow eggplant seeds, close the package carefully and put it into the refrigerator (or other cool, dry place), where they can remain viable for years. So many interesting eggplant varieties are available now: green ones the size and color of grapes, plump white ones, and long lavender types. Buy several different varieties and plan a garden of colorful, versatile eggplant.

Eggplant & Tomato Pasta Sauce

Four good things from your Square Foot garden—hot peppers, tomatoes, eggplant and basil—become a vibrant sauce for pasta.

1 medium eggplant, diced
3 tablespoons olive oil
1 small hot pepper, minced, or ½ teaspoon red pepper flakes
1 cup chopped fresh or canned tomatoes
Kosher salt
1 cup shredded mozzarella cheese
1 cup grated pecorino cheese
8 basil leaves, torn or sliced

Stir-fry the eggplant in the olive oil over high heat for 1 minute. Add the tomatoes and pepper and mix well. Reduce the heat to low, cover, and simmer for 15 to 20 minutes until the eggplant and tomato are very tender. Add the salt and mozzarella cheese and cook, stirring, until the cheese is melted. Serve the sauce over hot cooked pasta, topped with pecorino and basil. Makes 4 servings.

Mediterranean Eggplant Salad

Change up the flavor and texture by adding 2 cups of cooked, drained elbow macaroni or other pasta shape.

3 medium eggplants
1 small garlic clove, sliced
½ cup olive oil
3 tablespoons red wine vinegar
Salt and freshly ground pepper to taste
2 medium tomatoes, chopped
½ cup chopped cucumber
2 green onions, sliced
¼ cup chopped bell pepper
¼ cup chopped fresh parsley

Preheat the oven to 400 degrees. Oil the eggplant skins and roast for 40 minutes, turning once or twice, until collapsed. Let stand until cool enough to handle.

Combine the garlic and olive oil in a salad bowl. Add the vinegar and whisk to blend. Add salt and pepper. Peel the eggplants, discarding the skin. Add the eggplant to the dressing along with the tomatoes, cucumber, green onions, bell pepper and parsley. Mix well. Makes 4 generous servings.

Eggplant & Tomato Pasta Sauce

Classic Ratatouille

- 2 onions, finely chopped
- 2 tablespoons olive oil
- 2 medium eggplants, cut into 1-inch pieces
- 2 red bell peppers, chopped
- 4 tomatoes, chopped (peeled if you like)
- 2 garlic cloves, sliced
- 12 coriander seeds
- ½ cup chopped fresh basil and/or parsley

Sauté the onions in the olive oil in a large skillet or soup pan over low heat for 10 minutes until tender. Add the eggplant and bell pepper and stir to coat with the oil. Cover and cook for 30 minutes until very tender. Add the tomatoes, garlic and coriander seeds and cook for 10 to 15 minutes until the tomatoes fall apart, adding more oil as needed. Add the basil and parsley. Serve warm or at room temperature. Makes 4 large servings.

Herbed Eggplant Spread

Yogurt adds a creamy touch to this eastern Mediterranean snack. Use spearmint rather than peppermint leaves.

- 1 medium eggplant
- 1 bay leaf
- 1 branch thyme or ½ teaspoon dried thyme
- 1 large garlic clove, sliced
- 1 tablespoon olive oil
- 1 tablespoon fresh lemon juice
- ½ cup plain whole milk yogurt
- 2 tablespoons chopped fresh mint
- ½ teaspoon salt
- ¼ teaspoon freshly ground pepper

Preheat the oven to 400 degrees. Make several deep cuts in the eggplant. Stuff garlic, bay leaf and the thyme into the cuts. Bake for 45 minutes until the stem end is tender; let cool. Peel the eggplant and discard the stem, skin and bay leaf. Squeeze or drain any excess moisture in the flesh. Mash or purée the eggplant with the thyme and garlic.

Add the oil, lemon juice, yogurt, mint, salt and pepper; process or mix well. Let stand 30 minutes before serving at room temperature with crackers, bread or vegetables. Makes 1 cup.

Classic Ratatouille

Grill-Smoked Baba Ghanoush

This traditional Middle Eastern spread for pita bread is also a good topping for crostini and a dip for vegetables.

2 small eggplants
Oil or nonstick cooking spray
1 garlic clove, minced
2 to 3 tablespoons tahini paste
1 to 2 tablespoons lemon juice
½ teaspoon ground cumin
2 tablespoons minced fresh mint
2 tablespoons olive oil
Salt and freshly ground pepper to taste
Additional mint for garnish

Prepare a fire in a grill (or preheat the oven to 400 degrees). Coat the eggplants lightly with oil or nonstick cooking spray. Grill the eggplants, turning often, for 25 minutes (40 minutes in the oven) until the skins blacken and blister. Let cool slightly. Cut open the eggplants and scoop out the flesh, discarding the peel. Chop the eggplant and let it drain in a colander for a few minutes. Squeeze out the liquid.

Combine the eggplants, garlic, tahini, lemon juice, cumin, salt and pepper in a blender or food processor. Process the mixture until well blended and of a uniform texture. Stir in half of the mint. Spoon dip into a bowl and scatter remaining leaves and the olive oil on top. Makes 1½ cups or 12 (2-tablespoon) servings.

Eggplant Fries

This is a delicious way to enjoy eggplant—even if you don't usually enjoy eggplant.

1 medium eggplant
½ cup flour
⅔ cup cornstarch
¼ teaspoon salt
Dash of ground red pepper
Dash of garlic salt
½ cup vegetable oil
Seasoned salt

Peel the eggplant and cut into "fries." Combine the flour, cornstarch, salt, pepper and garlic salt in a paper or plastic bag, or a large bowl. Coat the eggplant "fries" in the flour mixture by shaking or rolling. Heat the oil to 365 to 375 degrees in a large skillet, wok or medium pot. Fry the eggplant until deep golden, working in batches if needed. Drain on paper towels. Sprinkle with seasoned salt. Makes 3 to 4 servings.

Creole Shrimp-Stuffed Eggplant

Oysters can be used in place of shrimp in this traditional Creole dish.

2 large eggplants
1 onion, minced
1 garlic clove, minced
1 green pepper, minced
2 celery ribs, minced
3 tablespoons butter
½ cup finely chopped parsley
½ teaspoon dried thyme
1 cup chopped cooked shrimp
Salt, freshly ground pepper and cayenne to taste
2 eggs
3 tablespoons butter, softened
½ cup seasoned bread crumbs
¼ cup Parmesan cheese

Cut the eggplants into halves lengthwise. Cut and scoop out the flesh, leaving a ¼ inch shell. Cook the flesh and shells in boiling water for 5 minutes; drain.

Sauté the onion, garlic, pepper and celery in half of the butter until tender. Add eggplant flesh, parsley, thyme, shrimp, salt and pepper and cayenne. Cook, stirring, for 3 minutes. Remove from the heat and stir in the eggs.

Preheat the oven to 350 degrees. Spoon the shrimp mixture into the shells. Combine the remaining butter with the bread crumbs and Parmesan cheese and sprinkle over each stuffed eggplant half. Bake for 20 minutes until heated through and browned. Makes 4 servings.

Grilled Pepper & Eggplant Sandwiches

2 large or 4 small sweet peppers, any color, cut into halves lengthwise
1 small eggplant, cut lengthwise into slices
4 whole small green onions
2 tablespoons olive oil
8 (½-inch) slices diagonally cut Italian or French bread
4 ounces soft goat cheese
2 tablespoons Dijon or grainy mustard

Brush or toss the pepper, eggplant and onion with oil. Grill or broil for 4 minutes, turn and grill for 3 to 5 minutes longer until peppers are charred in places, and onions and eggplant are tender. Cut the peppers and onions into strips. Spread one side of each French bread slice with goat cheese, then mustard. Layer eggplant slices and sweet pepper strips on four bread slices. Top with the remaining bread. Makes 4 sandwiches.

Taking the Harvest to the Table

Herbs

When to harvest

Parsley: Harvest the larger leaves at the outside of the plant first, leaving the new leaves to mature. **Basil:** Plants are ready beginning when they are six inches tall. **Mint:** Plants are ready beginning when they are six inches tall. **Dill:** Start picking the fresh leaves about midsummer, before the flowers appear.

Signs that it is ready

Parsley: Harvest parsley when it produces leaf stems with three segments. **Basil:** Pick basil leaves any time after the plant has reached six inches. **Mint:** Pick mint leaves any time after the plant has reached six inches. **Dill:** Dill fronds or fluffy clusters are ready to pick when they are one inch or longer. As the stems begin growing longer, pick more often to keep the plant producing.

When is it too late?

Parsley: You will have leaves until a heavy freeze. You can dig and pot parsley plants in the fall and bring them inside for a winter of pleasure. **Basil:** When the plant has produced seed from the tall flower shoots that form in the center of the plant, the plant puts out fewer, smaller leaves. **Mint:** Harvest before flowers form for best flavor. **Dill:** Once the plant produces flower heads,

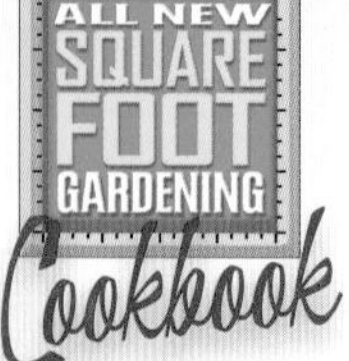

the production of leaves slows then stops. However, wait long enough and the seeds will fall to the ground and next year you will have dill plants everywhere.

How to harvest

Parsley: The leaves can be cut off individually, or cut a whole stem or two. **Basil:** Pinch off growing tips with your thumb and forefinger or clip them with scissors. Then prune the main stem from the top, leaving at least one node with two young shoots. Continue to cut back the branches, keeping the plant shaped in somewhat the same way you would keep a shrub trimmed. Always pinch off any flowers that appear to keep the plant producing new growth. **Mint:** Snip just above a cluster of leaves as needed. **Dill:** Cut off the fronds, or cut back the top of the plant to just above a frond. For dill seeds, cut the seed heads when the majority of seeds have formed, even if some flowers are still blooming. Hang the seed heads upside down in a paper bag to mature and dry out. The seeds will fall into the bag when they are ready.

Expected yield

Parsley: At four plants per square foot, you should have enough to pick daily for a healthier you. If eaten daily, people will start to ask you, "Are you working out now?" **Basil:** If you prune basil plants often, you can expect to get from fifteen to twenty cups of leaves from each plant over the season. The foliage from one full-size plant, dried and stored in an air-tight container, will yield a year's supply for most families. **Mint:** Same as basil. **Dill:** Yields are quite variable, depending on where and how plants are grown, and how often plants are harvested.

TIPS

Storage

Parsley: Store freshly picked parsley sprigs in the refrigerator with the stems in a jar of water covered with a plastic bag. Or sprinkle the leaves with water, put them in a plastic bag, and refrigerate. Parsley will keep in the refrigerator for up to two weeks. Parsley freezes well. Chop it and store in plastic bags. Or purée it with water in a blender and freeze in ice cube trays. Remove the frozen cubes and store in sealed plastic freezer bags. Frozen parsley will keep for six months. **Basil:** Stand basil stems in a jar of water and cover the foliage with a plastic bag (or it may turn black). To freeze basil, chop it and mix it with a little bit of olive oil and pack into plastic freezer bags. It also freezes well when ground and mixed with butter. Basil can be dried in a dehydrator or in the microwave oven, or you can air dry it in an area of low humidity on trays or screens. **Mint:** Chop and freeze in plastic bags or containers. Mint dries well, though it loses much of its flavor. Keep the leaves on the stems and dry them on screens or trays until the leaves feel stiff and dry. Crumble the leaves from the mint stems and dry them some more, then store in airtight jars. **Dill:** Stand dill stems in a jar of water, covered with a plastic bag. To freeze dill for longer storage, cut the leaves, stems and all, into sections short enough to fit into plastic freezer bags. (Do not chop the leaves into bits or fragrance and flavor will be lost.) It will keep in the freezer for six months. To dry dill, hang bunches of stems upside down in a dark, airy place until they are crumbly. Store them in a tightly sealed jar away from light and use within four to six months. For dried dill seed, cut the flowers when the seeds are brown but not yet dropping. Hang the dried flower heads in a paper bag until the seeds drop off.

KID'S CORNER

Name some of the herbs you know

1

2

3

4

5

Are you growing any of them? Taste one and describe its taste.

Draw a picture of the plant. Which part do we eat? What is the price of a small package of the herb from the grocery store?

Eat / Don't Eat

Parsley: Eat leaves and tender stems. Tough but flavorful stems can be used to flavor soups; remove them before serving. **Basil:** Leaves. **Mint:** Leaves. **Dill:** Leaves and seeds.

Companion Planting

Parsley: The plant helps repel carrot flies and protects roses against rose beetles. **Basil:** It helps tomatoes resist both insects and diseases, and when laid over tomatoes in a serving bowl will deter fruit flies. The Italians have been growing mint and basil with tomatoes for centuries. **Spearmint:** The plant repels ants.

Mel says . . .

Basil is just one pesto possibility. Sage, rosemary, cilantro, mint, lovage and parsley also make good pesto. Pesto keeps a couple of weeks in the refrigerator. For longer storage, freeze pesto in ice cube trays or mini muffin tins, then pop the cubes out and store in labeled plastic bags or rigid plastic freezer containers. Use to flavor braises, stews, soups, beans, pasta sauces, and vinaigrette.

Eight-Herb Butter Pasta

A fragrant and intensely flavorful pasta that uses a little of everything from the herb garden. Pair it with any pasta shape that has folds or hollows to hold the herb butter.

8 tablespoons (1 stick) butter
2 garlic cloves, minced
¼ to ½ teaspoon red pepper flakes
¼ cup olive oil or vegetable oil
¼ cup chopped basil
¼ cup chopped parsley
2 tablespoons sliced chives
2 tablespoons fennel tops or chervil
1 tablespoon chopped oregano
1 teaspoon chopped rosemary leaves
1 tablespoon chopped tarragon or lovage
1 teaspoon thyme leaves
Salt and freshly ground pepper to taste
1 pound hot cooked pasta, preferably bowties or orecchiete
Zest of 1 lemon, grated, optional
Grated Parmesan cheese to taste, optional

Heat the butter in a medium skillet over low heat. Add the garlic and pepper flakes and cook for 1 to 2 minutes. Add the herbs and cook, stirring, for 2 minutes or until they turn bright green. Pour the herb butter over the pasta. Toss to coat the pasta. Top with lemon and Parmesan if desired. Makes 4 servings.

Herb Toastlets

Just right for serving with soup. They can also be hors d'oeuvre—use a cutter to cut them into shapes. Toast them and top with a sliver of tomato, smoked salmon, or ham.

1 stick (8 tablespoons) butter, softened
½ cup minced mixed delicately flavored herbs (dill, parsley, watercress, fennel, chives, and chervil)
7 slices good-quality white bread

Preheat the oven to 400 degrees. Combine the butter and herbs in a bowl. Spread each piece of bread with the butter. Cut pieces into quarters or other shapes. Bake for 8 minutes or until sizzling and crisp. Serve warm. Makes 28 toast quarters.

Eight-Herb Butter Pasta

Green Goddess Dressing

When you taste Green Goddess Dressing made with fresh herbs, you discover how good this 1970s favorite can be. Update it by using olive oil in place of a portion of the mayonnaise and sour cream.

¼ cup mayonnaise
¼ cup sour cream
1 teaspoon lemon juice
1 teaspoon fish sauce or ½ inch anchovy paste
1 garlic clove
Salt and freshly ground pepper to taste
3 sliced green onions
½ cup parsley leaves
½ cup dill sprigs
20 fresh basil leaves
2 tablespoons white wine vinegar or lemon juice, optional

Combine the mayonnaise, sour cream, lemon juice, fish sauce, garlic, salt and pepper in a blender or food processor (or in a large bowl with a whisk); mix well. Add the onions, parsley, dill and basil and process briefly until well chopped. (Or mince the onions and herbs and stir them into the mayonnaise mixture.) Taste the dressing and add up to 2 tablespoons of vinegar. Makes about 1 cup, enough to dress 6 to 8 servings of salad.

Herbed Goat Cheese Spread

Imported herbed goat cheese costs a bundle at the store. Making your own gives you a fresher-tasting result, and you can customize the flavor with herbs.

2 garlic cloves, minced to a paste
5 to 8 ounces goat cheese, softened
8 ounces cream cheese, softened
½ cup chopped chives
½ cup chopped flat-leaf parsley
3 tablespoons minced basil, oregano or thyme leaves, or to taste

Combine the garlic, goat cheese and cream cheese in a small bowl and mix or beat well. Stir or beat in the herbs. Spoon the mixture into a crock, mold or small bowl. Refrigerate, covered, for 1 to 2 hours until firm. Keeps 1 week in the refrigerator. Makes about 2 cups.

Tarragon Chicken Salad

Tarragon's distinctive flavor is a great partner for mild chicken.

¼ cup mayonnaise
¼ cup sour cream
1 tablespoon tarragon vinegar or white wine vinegar
1 to 2 tablespoons chopped fresh tarragon
1 tablespoon chopped fresh chives
Salt and freshly ground pepper to taste
4 cups chopped cooked chicken
1 cup grape halves, optional
1 cup pecan pieces, divided
Salad greens or sliced tomatoes

Combine the mayonnaise, sour cream, vinegar, tarragon, chives, salt and pepper in a medium bowl and mix well. Add the chicken, grapes and ¾ cup of the pecans and mix well. Serve the chicken on salad greens or sliced tomatoes. Garnish with the remaining pecans. Makes 4 generous servings.

Chicken Herb Sauce for Polenta or Pasta

½ cup finely chopped onion
¼ cup chopped carrot
¼ cup minced parsley or lovage
2 tablespoons butter
2 tablespoons vegetable oil
1 pound ground chicken
Salt and freshly ground pepper to taste
1 tablespoon chopped fresh mint
⅔ cup dry white wine
2 large tomatoes, chopped, or 1 (15-ounce) can chopped tomatoes
1 teaspoon grated lemon peel
1 teaspoon minced sage
1 teaspoon minced rosemary
Grilled or fried polenta squares or hot cooked pasta

Sauté the onion, carrot and parsley in the butter and vegetable oil in a skillet over low heat for 10 minutes until very tender. Turn the heat to medium and add the chicken. Cook for 6 to 7 minutes, stirring, until chicken is cooked through and crumbly. Add the salt, pepper, mint and wine and cook for a few minutes until wine evaporates. Add the tomatoes and mix well. Reduce the heat to low and cook, covered, for about 25 minutes until the tomatoes completely lose their shape, stirring occasionally. Add the lemon peel, sage and rosemary and cook for 10 minutes longer to evaporate some of the liquid. Serve over polenta or pasta. Makes 4 servings.

Taking the Harvest to the Table

Salad Greens

When to harvest

These are cool-weather crops, so plant and eat a lot in the spring and fall. Continue picking until the plant flowers. Then pull the plant and replace it. Or, cut off the entire bunch of leaves at once about an inch above the ground. The remaining plant stub will produce new foliage in a few weeks. Harvest butter-head lettuce any time after the head reaches the size of your hand. Cut the loose head off each plant right at ground level. Harvest romaine lettuce when the leaves have elongated and overlapped to form a fairly tight head about three inches wide at the base and six to eight inches tall.

Signs that it is ready

Lettuce and spinach are ready for harvest when the outer leaves reach about three inches long.

When is it too late?

When the plant starts to "bolt," or send up a flower spike. This happens as weather turns hot.

How to harvest

Cut leaves from the plant with small scissors; cut whole heads at the base with a sharp knife.

Expected yield

HEAD LETTUCE: 4 heads per square foot.
LOOSE-LEAF LETTUCE: 6 bags per square foot.
SPINACH: 12 bags of leaves per square foot.

TIPS

Storage

Loose-leaf and butter-head lettuces taste best shortly after harvest. The excess keeps well in the refrigerator for one to two weeks if you harvest the leaves, roll them up in moistened, thick paper towels, and put them in an unsealed plastic bag or container. Crisp-head types will keep for about two weeks in the refrigerator. Use a lettuce spinner or paper towels to eliminate most of the moisture remaining from washing the lettuce before storing in the plastic bag or container. The lettuce will remain crisp for a longer time. Lettuce cannot be canned or frozen.

KID'S CORNER

Take or give a taste test of lettuce varieties. First, grow one square foot each of several types. Then test the flavors by color, leaf shape, and leaf size. Test the plants again as the leaves grow to determine whether the flavor changes with the leaf size. If you grow several lettuce types, you may find there's more flavor variety in lettuces than you thought. Be sure to note your favorites so you can grow them again next year, or later in the season as a fall crop.

Eat / Don't Eat

Leaves are edible. Head lettuces have an unappetizing core, and the stems of leaf lettuces are bitter and tough.

Companion Planting

Plant lettuces with beets and strawberries for a corner of the garden that's beautiful in the spring. It's nice next to dill, too. Planting lettuce alongside radishes produces radishes that are more tender. The lettuce controls flea beetles, too, which eat radishes and kohlrabi.

Mel says...

Even when greens are watered from below according to SFG method, they still get dirty and hold grit and dirt in their folds, so be sure to wash them well. Swish them in a sink or basin of water. You may have to handle each leaf individually if they're very dirty. At the very least it usually takes a second washing, so lift the greens out of the water before draining the sink. Rinse the dirt out of the sink and refill with fresh water.

Mixed Lettuces, Mango & Avocado with Lime Honey Dressing

A sweet-tangy dressing and a touch of mango give this salad a real flavor difference.

Lime Honey Dressing

1 teaspoon grated lime peel
Juice of 1 lime
3 tablespoons honey
2 tablespoons vegetable oil

Salad

3 cups torn or chopped romaine lettuce
3 cups torn soft lettuce leaves
3 green onions, sliced
1 avocado, pitted, sliced or cubed
1 mango or tomato, peeled, pitted, cubed
Toasted tortilla strips

For the dressing, combine the lime peel, lime juice, honey and vegetable oil in a serving bowl with a fork or whisk and mix well. Add the lettuces, onions and avocado and toss to coat. Top with the mango and tortilla strips. Makes 6 side dish servings.

Arugula & Chervil Salad

Chervil's delicate parsley-fennel flavor deserves wider appreciation. Its small leaves need no chopping—they can go directly into salad, spreads or on top of cooked foods. Here, it adds a sweet note to the powerful combination of arugula, lemon and aged cheese.

Rosemary Lemon Vinaigrette (page 22)
4 handfuls arugula leaves
1 handful chervil tops
4 basil leaves
2/3 cup shaved white Cheddar or aged gouda

Pile the arugula, chervil and basil onto a cutting board. Chop coarsely into bite-size pieces. Put into a serving bowl or divide between individual bowls. (Or refrigerate for later.) Dress with Rosemary Lemon Vinaigrette and toss to coat. Arrange cheese on top. Makes 4 small servings.

Mixed Lettuces...with Lime Honey Dressing

Asian Chicken Lettuce Wraps

A delicious copycat of a popular restaurant entrée. If you're uncomfortable deep-frying the noodles, cook them by the package directions instead and drain very well, then chop or snip the noodles into 1- to 2-inch lengths. The finished wraps will still be delicious.

Chicken and marinade

1 teaspoon cornstarch
2 teaspoons sherry or rice wine
2 teaspoons water
2 teaspoons soy sauce
1 teaspoon vegetable oil
3 cups chopped or ground chicken breast meat

Hoisin Sesame Cooking Sauce

2 tablespoons hoisin sauce
2 tablespoons oyster sauce
1 teaspoon sesame oil
1 tablespoon soy sauce
1 tablespoon dry sherry or rice wine
2 tablespoons water
1 teaspoon sugar
2 teaspoons cornstarch

Filling

1/3 cup vegetable oil or peanut oil
1 teaspoon grated or minced fresh ginger
2 teaspoons minced garlic
6 green onions, sliced
1 cup chopped mushrooms
1 (8-ounce) can water chestnuts, minced
1 (6-ounce) package cellophane noodles, deep-fried until crisp
8 to 10 large leaves soft lettuce

Combine the cornstarch, wine, water, soy sauce, oil and chicken in a bowl and mix well.

Mix all ingredients for hoisin sesame cooking sauce and set aside.

Heat a wok or large skillet over medium-high heat. Add 3 tablespoons of the oil. Stir-fry the chicken for 3 to 5 minutes just until cooked through. Remove the chicken from the skillet.

Heat 2 more tablespoons of the oil. Add the ginger, garlic and green onions and stir-fry for 1 minute. Add the mushrooms and water chestnuts and stir-fry for 2 minutes. Return the chicken to the pan. Stir the cooking sauce and add to the pan. Cook, stirring, until thickened and hot. Spoon into a serving bowl. Break the cellophane noodles into shorter lengths. Top the chicken mixture with the noodles.

Serve with the lettuce leaves. Spoon some of the mixture into a lettuce leaf and roll, burrito-style, to enclose the filling. Makes enough for 8 to 10 rolls.

Asian Chicken Lettuce Wraps

Escarole Salad with Lemon Pear Dressing

Any slightly bitter green will work for this salad—besides escarole, you can use sliced endive, chicory, arugula, tender mustard greens or young kale.

- 2 handfuls chicory or escarole, torn into bite-size pieces
- 2 handfuls tender lettuce leaves
- 4 or 5 radishes, trimmed, sliced
- 2 tablespoons white wine vinegar
- ½ very ripe, soft pear, peeled, cored
- 1 tablespoon lemon juice
- 1 tablespoon balsamic vinegar
- 1 tablespoon vegetable oil, or more as needed
- Salt and freshly ground pepper to taste

Combine the chicory, lettuce and radishes in a serving bowl. Purée the pear. Add the lemon juice, balsamic vinegar, vegetable oil and salt and pepper and process until well mixed. Add more oil to make the dressing of a pourable consistency. Pour the dressing over the salad; toss to combine. Makes 4 servings.

Arugula & Potato Salad

Arugula is such a rewarding crop—just scatter the seeds over a square foot after the first frost and you'll have weeks of tasty young greens for salad and older, spicier greens for other uses.

- 1 pound new potatoes, cut into chunks
- Shallot Vinaigrette, page 132
- 2 generous handfuls arugula, washed and well dried
- ¼ cup thinly sliced basil

Combine the potatoes and water to cover in a saucepan. Simmer for 8 minutes or until the potatoes are tender; drain. Combine with ⅓ cup of the dressing. Arrange the arugula on a serving platter or in a bowl. Top with the potatoes, then sprinkle with the basil. Makes 4 servings.

Persian Herbs & Greens Oven Omelet

A nice way to use lettuce and other tender greens when you've had enough salad. Adding the baking soda and yogurt produces a puffed, soufflé-like texture, and omitting them yields a texture more like a quiche.

2 tablespoons vegetable oil
1 cup shredded tender arugula, chard or spinach
8 leaves red- or green-leaf lettuce or romaine, torn or shredded
½ cup chopped fresh parsley
2 tablespoons chopped fresh dill
6 green onions, sliced
4 garlic cloves, minced
2 teaspoons all-purpose flour
2 tablespoons water
6 to 8 eggs
½ cup chopped walnuts or pistachios, optional
½ teaspoon ground cardamom
Salt and freshly ground pepper to taste
¼ teaspoon baking soda, optional
2 tablespoons plain yogurt or sour cream, optional
½ cup goat cheese, optional

Preheat oven to 325 degrees. Pour the oil into a 10-inch skillet with an ovenproof handle and set it in the oven to heat.

Combine the arugula, lettuce, parsley, dill, green onions and garlic in a large bowl.

Combine the flour and water in a medium bowl and mix well. Whisk in the eggs, walnuts, cardamom, salt and pepper and mix well. Whisk in the baking soda and yogurt. Stir in the cheese. Pour the egg mixture over the lettuce mixture and mix lightly.

Pour the egg mixture into the hot skillet. Bake for 35 to 40 minutes until eggs are set and top is browned. Makes 4 servings.

Fried Halloumi Salad with Caper Vinaigrette

Halloumi cheese is usually available at markets with a good selection of Middle Eastern groceries. It remains firm when cooked or grilled.

Caper Vinaigrette

Zest and juice of 1 lemon
2 tablespoons olive oil
1 teaspoon Dijon mustard
1 tablespoon balsamic vinegar
1 to 2 teaspoons capers
1 garlic clove, minced
1 shallot, minced
2 tablespoons chopped fresh parsley
Salt and freshly ground pepper to taste

Salad

8 to 10 ounces halloumi cheese
½ to ⅔ cup all-purpose flour
Salt and pepper to taste
2 tablespoons oil
4 to 5 cups chopped romaine lettuce or torn green- and red-leaf lettuces

For the dressing, combine the lemon zest and juice, olive oil, mustard, vinegar, capers, garlic, shallot, parsley, salt and pepper in a jar with a tight-fitting lid and shake to blend. Alternatively, mix in a bowl with a fork.

For the salad, pat the cheese dry and cut into 8 slices. Combine the flour, salt and pepper on a plate or waxed paper. Coat the cheese with the flour mixture. Fry in the oil in a skillet over medium-high heat for a few minutes until golden.

Arrange the salad greens in the bowl; add the dressing and toss to combine. Top with the warm cheese. Drizzle with more vinaigrette. Makes 2 main dish or 4 side salads.

Main Dish Spinach Salad with Smoky Bacon Dressing

The dressing makes enough to dress eight ounces of spinach—just keep tossing.

10 ounces good-quality smoked bacon
2 (8-ounce) packages fresh button mushrooms
½ cup vegetable oil
1 red onion, sliced into rings
2 shallots, sliced
1 tablespoon sugar
1 tablespoon ketchup, fruit syrup or preserves
2 tablespoons cider vinegar
Salt and freshly ground pepper to taste
4 to 8 ounces fresh spinach (depending on how many you're feeding)
1 cup sliced almonds, toasted

Cook the bacon in a skillet over medium-high heat until it reaches your preferred doneness. Drain on paper towel. Chop or crumble the bacon. Drain all but 2 tablespoons of the bacon grease. Heat it to medium and sauté the mushrooms, covered, until they release some of their liquid. Remove with a slotted spoon.

Add 2 tablespoons of vegetable oil to the liquid in the skillet and sauté the onions and shallots until they are tender. Reduce the heat to low. Add the ketchup and sugar and cook, covered, for 15 minutes until the onions are deep brown. Add the vinegar and cook, stirring, until well blended. Add the remaining vegetable oil and mix well.

Arrange the spinach in a serving bowl. Top with the mushrooms, then the almonds. Pour (or spoon—it may be too thick to pour) the dressing and onions over the salad. Toss and toss—it will eventually coat every leaf. Top with the bacon. Makes 4 to 6 generous servings.

Taking the Harvest to the Table

Melons & Berries

Signs that it is ready

Cantaloupe and other melons with a net pattern outside are easy to judge—the netting becomes more pronounced and turns a tan color. Both cantaloupe and honeydews are ripe when the fruit slips off the vine easily. They do not continue to ripen after being picked. That's why you should grow your own. Strawberries are ready to harvest when they are completely red, not green at the tip. Raspberries and blackberries are ripe when they slide right off the plant into your hand.

When is it too late?

It is too late to pick melons when they become mushy or fall from the vine. That's a no-brainer, isn't it?

How to harvest

Press the base of the melon stem with your thumb. A ripe melon will slip right off. Pick raspberries and blackberries at least twice a week when they are bearing. Be careful not to squeeze the berries; just lift them off the stem gently. Strawberries can be hard to find. Lift up the leaves to find the berries hiding underneath. Since strawberries are easily bruised, use two hands and pinch the stem with a fingernail, or cut the stem with your garden scissors, instead of pulling the berry.

Expected yield

Each strawberry plant should produce almost a quart over the harvest season.

TIPS

■ *Storage*

Cantaloupe-type melons may keep for a week in a cool place, while casabas can last for as long as several weeks. Strawberries, raspberries, and blackberries store well in the refrigerator in small containers for about a week at the most.

■ *Eat / Don't Eat*

Melon and berry fruits are edible.

■ *Companion Planting*

Rotating crops—planting something different in each square each year—is a good plan for soil and garden health, but remember that melon, squash, and cucumber all are in the same family when you're making your rotation chart. Plant strawberries with spinach—they go well together in a salad and are ready at the same time.

KID'S CORNER

Keep a daily record of the high and low temperatures, the date, and the growth of different plants. For example, once melons have formed their flower, become pollinated, and started with a small melon shape, it could be flagged, so you go back to the same one every time, and then measure the length or circumference. The next step would be to not only take those recordings and compare them with other vegetable records, but then depending on your interest, plot them on a chart or a graph.

Mel says...

If you're going to grow melons vertically, start with smaller varieties as you learn how to train the vines up the trellis. The jumbo varieties may need extra support so the larger fruits won't break loose and fall to the ground. This is especially true for watermelons, but also of all melons and especially vertically grown pumpkins.

Watermelon Wave

A refreshing drink that is great for snack time.

8 cups deseeded watermelon chunks
¼ to ⅔ cup superfine sugar
Juice of 1 lime or 2 ounces (4 tablespoons) frozen limeade concentrate
2 to 3 cups crushed ice
½ cup water, if needed

Combine the watermelon, sugar and lime juice in a blender or food processor. Process until smooth. Add the ice and process until mixture is uniformly frosted. Add the water if the mixture becomes too thick to process. Spoon or pour into glasses to serve. Makes 6 small servings.

Watermelon Cake with Watermelon Frosting

An unusual and surprising dessert that's a light finish for summer meals.

Cake
1 (18-ounce) box white cake mix
1 (3-ounce) package mixed fruit or strawberry-kiwi gelatin
1 tablespoon flour
¾ cup vegetable oil
4 eggs
1 cup chopped watermelon

Watermelon Frosting
8 tablespoons (1 stick) butter or margarine, softened
1 (16-ounce) box confectioners' sugar
¼ cup puréed watermelon
Red food coloring
Semisweet chocolate morsels

For the cake, preheat the oven to 325 degrees. Combine the cake mix, gelatin and flour in a bowl. Add the oil, eggs and melon. Beat with an electric mixer until well blended. Divide the batter between two greased and floured 8-inch cake pans. Bake for 30 minutes. Cool in the pans 2 minutes. Remove and cool completely.

For the frosting, stir or beat together the butter and sugar. Add a few drops of food coloring and enough of the watermelon to make the frosting a spreadable consistency. Use the frosting to fill and frost the cake layers. Decorate the top with chocolate chips for "seeds." Makes 16 servings.

Watermelon Wave

Blueberry Fool

Use any berry or a mixture for this creamy dessert, but stick with one or two varieties to keep the resulting color pure and attractive. The recipe halves well, in case you have just a handful of berries.

1 cup heavy whipping cream
1 cup sour cream or crème fraiche
2 cups berries
¼ cup sugar
1 tablespoon orange juice, raspberry liqueur or orange liqueur
1 tablespoon strawberry jam or jelly, optional
4 small berries for garnish

Combine the whipping cream and sour cream in a medium bowl and mix well.

Combine the berries, sugar, orange juice, and jam in a blender or food processor; process until smooth and well blended. Fold the cream mixture into the berry mixture until no streaks of cream or fruit purée are visible. Spoon into custard cups, martini glasses or parfait glasses. Garnish each serving with a berry. Makes 4 servings.

Watermelon Mint Feta Salad

Vary the flavor by using a few basil leaves as well as mint leaves.

1/3 cup fresh mint leaves, chopped
2 tablespoons fresh lime juice
2 tablespoons virgin olive oil
6 cups watermelon, seeded, diced, chilled
½ cup crumbled feta cheese
Freshly ground pepper
Cayenne pepper, optional

Combine the mint leaves, lime juice and olive oil in a small bowl and whisk to blend. Just before serving, pour the mixture over the melon in a serving bowl, tossing to coat. Top with the cheese, then season with pepper. Makes 6 servings.

Blueberry Fool

Berry Crunch Coffeecake

Cake

¾ cup all-purpose flour
¾ cup whole wheat flour
¾ cup raw sugar or brown sugar
2 teaspoons baking powder
½ teaspoon salt
¼ cup vegetable oil
1 egg
½ cup milk
¾ cup blackberries, strawberries or blueberries, fresh or frozen

Topping

1/3 cup raw sugar or brown sugar
1 tablespoon whole wheat flour or unbleached white flour
1 tablespoon rolled oats
1 teaspoon ground cinnamon
1/3 cup chopped pecans, walnuts or hazelnuts
2 tablespoons softened butter

For the cake, preheat the oven to 375 degrees. Combine the flours, sugar, baking powder and salt in a bowl. Beat the oil, egg and milk in a medium bowl. Add the oil mixture to the dry ingredients; beat just until blended. Pour the batter into a greased 9-inch baking pan. Spread the berries over the batter.

Combine the topping ingredients in a blender or food processor; process until the oats and nuts are finely chopped and the mixture holds together in clumps. Crumble the mixture over the cake. Bake for 25 to 35 minutes or until the center is set. Cool for 30 minutes to 1 hour before cutting in the pan. Makes 8 servings.

Strawberry Lemonade & Freezer Pops

3 cups cold water
4 cups strawberries
¾ cup sugar
¾ cup lemon juice
2 cups cold club soda

Combine water, strawberries, sugar and lemon juice in a blender. Process until smooth. Add the soda and process briefly to mix. Serve right away in glasses, garnished with mint, lemon or a strawberry, if desired.

For ice pops, spoon the mixture into ice pop molds. Insert handles or wooden sticks and freeze. Makes 4 drinks or 16 small ice pops.

Fresh Strawberry Bread

Berries that are bruised or overripe are ideal for Strawberry Bread because they'll be puréed or mashed, so looks don't matter.

- 1½ cups unbleached white flour
- ½ teaspoon baking soda
- 1 teaspoon cinnamon
- ⅛ teaspoon salt
- 2 eggs
- 1 cup sugar
- ½ cup vegetable oil
- 1 teaspoon vanilla extract
- 1½ cups sliced strawberries
- ½ cup chopped pecans or walnuts, optional

Preheat the oven to 350 degrees. Stir together the flour, baking soda, cinnamon and salt in a large bowl. Beat the eggs and sugar in a medium bowl until well blended. Add the oil and vanilla; beat very well. Pour the egg mixture into the flour mixture and mix until only a few streaks of dry flour are visible.

Process the strawberries briefly in a blender or food processor, or mash with a potato masher. They should have some texture but no big chunks. Fold the strawberries and pecans into the batter until no streaks of strawberry purée remain.

Spoon the batter into a greased 8- to 9-inch loaf pan. Bake for 45 minutes, then check for doneness. Bake for 10 minutes longer if needed. Cool in the pan for 2 minutes, then remove and cool almost completely before slicing. Makes 1 loaf, about 16 slices.

Mixed Melons with Ginger Lime Syrup

- 1 tablespoon grated lime zest
- 1 slice fresh ginger, about the size of a quarter
- ¼ teaspoon ground cardamom, or 10 cardamom seeds
- ⅓ cup fresh lime juice
- ⅓ cup water
- ⅔ cup sugar
- 8 cups cubed watermelon, cantaloupe and/or honeydew

Combine the lime zest, ginger, cardamom, lime juice, water and sugar in a small saucepan or microwavable bowl. Simmer or microwave, stirring occasionally, until the sugar is dissolved. Simmer for 1 minute longer. Remove from the heat and let stand until cool. Discard the ginger slice (and the cardamom seeds). Chill the syrup in the refrigerator.
Pour the cold syrup over the melon in a serving bowl. Serve chilled or at room temperature. Makes 8 servings.

Taking the Harvest to the Table

Peas

When to harvest

Pick peas promptly. Pea vines produce from the bottom up so look for ripe peas at the bottom first. As soon as you pick peas, the sugar in them begins turning to starch, so for the sweetest peas, pick when you are ready to eat or store them. Be sure to pick plants often to keep the vines producing.

Signs that it is ready

Pick green peas when you can feel the peas inside the pods but they do not feel hard. You can also open a pod and taste the peas. Edible-pod peas are very different and are picked before the peas form, when the pods are full size but still flat. Sugar snap peas can be picked when the peas are already formed and will still be sweet and tender.

When is it too late?

When the peas in the pod feel hard, they are no longer edible. Add them to the compost pile or feed them to chickens—nothing is too tough for them.

How to harvest

Pick peas with two hands. Hold the vine with one hand, and pick off the pods with the other. Or, use that important SFG tool, your garden scissors. That way, you are assured you won't harm the vines.

TIPS

KID'S CORNER

Peas are a good subject for determining the yield of a plant. You can usually count the seeds through the pod. Keep a record of the number of pea pods and the number of peas in the pod and multiply those two numbers to get the total number of peas from each plant. Peas are good for saving for seed, too. Tie a piece of colored string around a stem to mark it. Leave that pod on the bush or vine until the peas get very large and the pod turns yellow-brown. Remove the seeds from the shell and save them to plant next year. See how well they grow compared to seed packets you buy.

- ***Storage***

  Peas are best eaten the day they are picked. If this isn't possible, put them in the refrigerator or freezer right away. Peas freeze well, retaining their sweet taste.

- ***Eat / Don't Eat***

  Eat edible-pod peas like tender green beans, pod and all. Green peas must be removed from the pod before eating. That used to be called shelling the peas in the good ole days.

- ***Companion Planting***

  Plant peas with carrots, turnips, radishes, cucumbers, corn, beans, potatoes, aromatic herbs. Peas do not grow well with onions, garlic, and gladiolus. Rotate peas with broccoli, cabbage, cauliflower, lettuce, root crops, or spinach.

Mel says...

There are so many pea varieties with so many different characteristics. Read seed catalogs and select carefully and you could be growing peas that don't need support, peas with abundant edible shoots, or peas with extra long pods. That's like getting more food for no extra work!

Pea Risotto

If you have a pressure cooker, you can make risotto in eight minutes without all the stirring. Just sauté the rice, then add all the broth at once, stir a few times, and lock on the lid. Once the valve begins to rock, cook for eight minutes, then quick-release the pressure according to the manufacturer's directions.

- 6 cups chicken broth or vegetable broth
- 2 cups peas or sugar snaps
- 1 onion, finely chopped
- 3 tablespoons butter
- 2 garlic cloves, minced
- 2 tablespoons olive oil
- 1½ cups Arborio rice
- 1½ teaspoons salt
- ⅔ cup grated Parmesan cheese
- Freshly ground black pepper

Warm the broth in a saucepan and keep it at a simmer. Measure ½ cup of the broth into another saucepan and cook the peas in it for a minute or two; set aside off the heat.

Sauté the onion in the butter in a heavy-bottomed 3-quart saucepan, flameproof casserole or Dutch oven over medium heat for 8 minutes until the onion is tender. Add the garlic and sauté for 2 minutes. Add the olive oil and sauté the rice for 2 to 3 minutes until all the grains are coated with butter and oil. Add ½ to ⅓ cup of the broth and cook, stirring, until most of the liquid is absorbed but not until rice is cooked dry. Continue adding broth and cooking until the rice absorbs most of it.

When the rice has cooked for 20 minutes, add the peas and their liquid. Cook, stirring, until the broth is mostly absorbed. Test the rice for doneness—it should be cooked through but firm, in a creamy, almost souplike liquid. It may need more broth and 5 additional minutes of cooking.

Add the salt and cheese and mix well. Remove from the heat and add the pepper. Spoon into soup bowls to serve. Makes 4 to 6 servings.

Pea Risotto

Creamy Pea or Sugar Snap Soup

- ½ cup chopped shallot or onion
- 2 tablespoons butter
- 2 tablespoons flour
- 2 cups chicken broth
- Salt to taste
- 2 cups shelled peas or sugar snaps
- 1 cup half-and-half
- White pepper to taste
- Sliced green onions for garnish

Sauté the onion in the butter in a soup pan over medium heat for 10 minutes until tender. Add the flour and mix well. Stir in the chicken broth, salt and peas. Cook, stirring, until mixture is thickened. Cook for 15 minutes longer. Purée the mixture. If you used sugar snaps, strain the mixture to remove any tough skin.

Return the purée to the pan. Add the half-and-half and mix well. Cook until heated through. Season with white pepper. Serve warm, garnished with green onions. Or chill and serve cold with a spoonful of sour cream. Makes 2 to 3 servings.

Snow Pea or Sugar Snap Stir-Fry

Light flavors let the peas' fresh taste shine.

- 1½ cup water
- 1½ teaspoons cornstarch
- ¼ teaspoon chicken bouillon granules
- 1 tablespoon soy sauce
- 2 tablespoons vegetable oil
- 2 cups snow peas or sugar snaps
- 1½ cups sliced shiitake mushrooms

Combine the water, cornstarch, bouillon granules and soy sauce in a small bowl and mix well.

Heat a large skillet or wok over high heat. Add the oil. Stir-fry the snow peas and mushrooms in oil for 2 minutes until both are crisp-tender.

Add the cornstarch mixture to the skillet. Cook, stirring, until the mixture thickens and boils. Makes 3 to 4 servings.

Creamy Pea or Sugar Snap Soup

Herb Cheese-Stuffed Snow Peas

For a really memorable hors d'oeuvre, press a small cooked shrimp into the herbed cheese.

30 snow peas or sugar snaps
About ⅓ cup homemade herbed goat cheese (page 80) or boursin cheese
Tiny dill, thyme or fennel sprigs

Steam or boil the snow peas in boiling water for 30 seconds; drain. Chill in ice water to stop the cooking. Drain very well and pat dry.

Cut the pea pods open with a small, sharp knife. Spoon or pipe herbed cheese into the peas. Garnish with a dill sprig. Arrange on a serving platter. Makes 30 hors d'oeuvres.

Crunchy Pea & Peanut Salad

If you gather your snow peas when they are young and tender, use them raw. Otherwise, steam them for just 1 minute or so.

2 cups snow peas or sugar snaps, cut into bite-size pieces
1 cup chopped cauliflower
1 cup sliced celery or ¼ cup chopped lovage
1 cup finely chopped sweet banana pepper or bell pepper
¼ cup sliced green onions
1 cup Shallot Vinaigrette (page 132), Chive Vinaigrette (page 112) or bottled Italian dressing
½ cup sour cream
¼ cup minced fresh dill
Salt and pepper to taste
1 cup unsalted roasted peanuts or cashews, roughly chopped

Combine the snow peas, cauliflower, celery, pepper and onions in a serving bowl. Combine the vinaigrette, sour cream, dill, salt and pepper in a small bowl with a whisk or fork; mix until well blended. Pour the dressing over the vegetables; toss to combine. When ready to serve, sprinkle the peanuts over the dressing. Makes 6 to 8 servings.

Pasta with Peas, Asparagus & Cream

A good recipe for the times when just a handful of asparagus and peas are ripe.

12 asparagus spears, trimmed, cut into 1-inch lengths
16 sugar snaps
2 garlic cloves, sliced or minced
2 tablespoons olive oil
1 tablespoon white wine, optional
12 medium shrimp, shelled
3 tablespoons heavy cream
4 to 6 ounces (2 to 3 servings) hot cooked pasta
Coarse salt, freshly ground pepper and fresh chives to taste

Steam or microsteam the asparagus and sugar snaps for 2 minutes. Let stand for 2 minutes. Chill in ice water to stop the cooking.

Sauté the garlic in the oil in a medium skillet over medium-low heat until fragrant. Turn the heat to medium, add the wine, and sizzle until mostly evaporated. Add the shrimp and cook, turning once, just until pink, about 1 minute on each side. Add the cream and cook until heated through.

Combine the shrimp mixture, pasta, asparagus, sugar snaps, salt, pepper and chives in a large bowl and mix well. Makes 3 generous servings.

Basil-Scented Zucchini & Pea Sauté

Every good cook needs a few quick, easy vegetable side dishes that everyone seems to like.

2 medium zucchini
1 tablespoon olive oil
1 tablespoon vegetable oil
1 cup fresh peas
Salt to taste
6 to 8 basil leaves, torn
2 mint leaves, torn

Cut the zucchini into quarters lengthwise, then slice. Heat the oils in a large sauté pan. Add the zucchini, peas, salt, half of the basil and a couple tablespoons of water. Cook over medium-low heat, stirring occasionally, for 5 minutes or until tender. Add the remaining basil and mint. Makes 2 large or 4 small servings.

Onions, Garlic & Chives

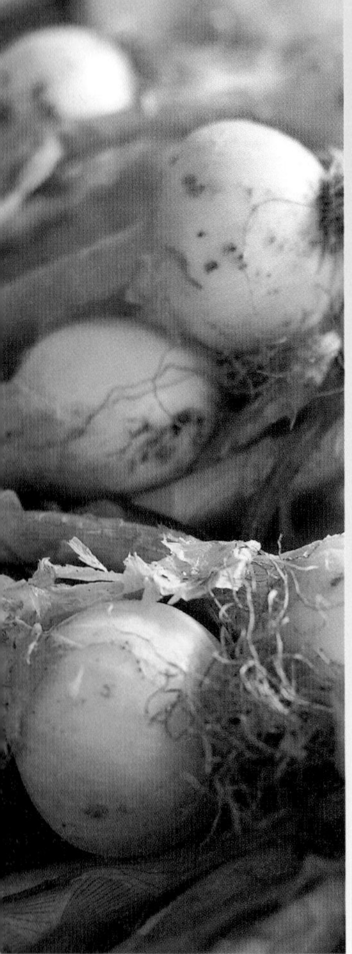

When to harvest

Onions: All types of bulbing onions can be eaten as scallions (spring onions) before bulbing begins, or after they are mature. **Chives:** Snip leaves anytime you need them. They will keep growing for many more harvests. **Garlic:** The curlicue green stems called "scapes" can be cut when tender and stir-fried like green onions. Garlic bulbs can be harvested before maturity for salads or stir-fries, or wait until they are mature for best storage quality.

Signs that it is ready

Onions: When about half the tops have fallen over, push over the rest then wait a few days and pull the onions from the earth. Let them sit in the sun for a few days before storing. **Chives:** Chives can be snipped once the leaves are a few inches tall. Don't remove more than one-third of the plant at any one time. **Garlic:** It's harvest time when the heads have segmented into cloves and the tops have turned color and fallen over.

When is it too late?

Onions: If an onion plant starts to send up a flower stalk, harvest it and use it immediately. **Chives:** It's never too late to snip some chive leaves. **Garlic:** Once the heads begin to burst open, they won't store well.

How to harvest

Onions: Loosen the soil around the bulbs and gently pull them from the ground. Let them lie on dry soil in the sun to cure for a few days. If the soil is wet or rain is forecast, bring the onions indoors, spread them on a tarp or newspaper and allow them to dry until the tops have completely shriveled. **Chives**: Snip off the tips of the leaves as needed. **Garlic:** Dig the plants when the cloves have fully segmented but before the heads begin to split open. Shake off the soil and spread them out under cover in the shade. Let them dry for two or three days, then peel a layer or two off the bulbs to remove any remaining soil. Let them continue to dry until the leaves shrivel, then clip them off about an inch above the bulb.

KID'S CORNER

Ask your folks about how many onions a week or month your family uses. Turn that into a total for the year. If you can grow sixteen onions in a square foot, how many square feet will you need to produce a year's worth of onions for your family?

Expected yield

Onions and garlic yield sixteen plants per square foot, while four to nine individual chive plants will eventually spread and fill the square foot for a bountiful, continuous harvest. In many parts of the country, chives survive over the winter and are the first plant ready to harvest next spring.

TIPS

Storage

Keep onions cool, dry, and separated from each other. Let the tops dry until the necks of the onions are thin and brown. Hang onions in mesh onion bags. Onions can be stored in the refrigerator wrapped individually in foil for up to one year. Onions can also be pickled.

Chives are best fresh. You can chop the leaves and freeze them in plastic bags, or make and freeze chive butter. Chives can also be chopped and dried. In fact, think of what a great gift some sun-dried chives would make.

When garlic leaves are completely shriveled, braid them together, or cut the leaves off an inch above the bulb. Garlic bulbs can also be hung in a mesh onion bag.

Eat / Don't Eat

Young onion bulbs and leaves are edible. Mature onion bulbs and garlic heads are edible. The leaves of chives are edible.

Mel says . . .

In India and other parts of the world, gardeners planted large bulb onions touching each other. The tops were cut for soups and stews, and the onion bulb sprouted another group of leaves! This can go on for at least three or four cycles before the bottoms are spent. I saw it when I visited India, and it worked well.

Grilled Sweet Onion Packets

Choose one of the supersweet onion varieties, such as Oso, Walla Walla, Maui or Vidalia.

1 onion per person
1 tablespoon butter per serving
1 beef bouillon cube, or 1 teaspoon bouillon granules, per serving
Freshly ground pepper to taste

Prepare a fire in a grill. Peel the onions and cut off the ends. Cut out some of the inside at the top of each onion to make room for the bouillon cube and butter. Insert the bouillon cube, then top with the butter. Wrap the onion in two layers of aluminum foil. Set it over indirect heat on the grill. Grill for 1 hour, or until onion is tender all the way through. Makes variable servings.

Whole Roasted Garlic

Whole heads of roasted garlic make delicious salad dressing and add a wonderful flavor to everything from mayonnaise to baked chicken to mashed potatoes.

6 mature heads garlic, cured until the skins are papery
Oil or nonstick cooking spray

Preheat the oven to 375 degrees. Peel off the outside layer of skin, leaving the cloves intact. Lightly oil a large square of aluminum foil. Arrange the garlic heads on the foil and seal tightly. Bake for 40 minutes to 1 hour, until garlic paste squeezes from each clove when it is pinched. Store in the refrigerator for up to 2 weeks. Makes 6 garlic heads.

To freeze, combine the garlic with enough vegetable oil to give it a "spreadable" consistency in a food processor. Pulse a few times to blend. Spoon the garlic mixture into a plastic storage bag. Flatten and freeze. Break off portions as needed.

Garlic & Chive Mashed Potatoes

1½ pounds Idaho (baking) potatoes, peeled, cut into chunks
3 cups water
3 chicken bouillon cubes
5 garlic cloves, peeled, left whole
5 tablespoons cream cheese
1 tablespoon snipped fresh chives
3 tablespoons butter
1 teaspoon salt

Combine the potatoes, water, bouillon cubes and garlic in a saucepan. Bring to a boil over high heat. Reduce the heat and cover. Simmer the potatoes for 10 to 15 minutes or until tender. Drain, reserving 1 cup of the cooking liquid.

Mash the potatoes and garlic or beat with an electric mixer until mashed. Add the cream cheese and chives and mix well.

Beat in enough of the reserved cooking liquid to make potatoes light and fluffy. Add the butter and salt and mix well. Makes 4 servings.

Garlic & Rosemary Baked Feta

1 (8-ounce) block feta cheese
¼ cup olive oil
3 garlic cloves, minced
1 teaspoon freshly cracked black pepper
1 tablespoon rosemary leaves

Preheat the oven to 400 degrees. Set the cheese in a small, preferably shallow, baking dish. Pour the oil over the cheese. Top the cheese with the garlic, pepper and rosemary. Bake for 15 to 20 minutes until the oil is bubbly. Serve with bread or crackers. Makes 8 (2-tablespoon) servings.

Chive Vinaigrette

¼ cup red wine vinegar
2 teaspoons sugar, optional
2 tablespoons minced fresh chives
2 teaspoons Dijon mustard
½ cup vegetable oil
Salt and freshly ground pepper to taste

Combine the vinegar, sugar and chives in a jar with a tight-fitting lid; shake to mix. Add the Dijon mustard and shake well. Add the oil, salt and pepper and shake well. Store in the refrigerator for up to three weeks. Makes 1 scant cup.

Garlic & Chive Mashed Potatoes

Caramelized Onions with a Balsamic Variation

Homegrown onions have a shorter storage life than commercially grown and processed onions. When your onions need attention, caramelize them in a big batch. They're ready to use when they're deep golden and glazed. Go a step further and add a spoonful or two of balsamic vinegar for another layer of flavor and to help them keep for 10 days in the refrigerator. Use them on pizza or bruschetta, with meats, as a topping for burgers, pasta, and more.

- 3 tablespoons olive oil
- 8 onions, sliced into rings
- Salt
- Water
- 3 tablespoons balsamic vinegar, optional

Heat the oil in a large skillet or Dutch oven over medium heat. Add the onions, salt them lightly, and cover the pan. Cook, covered and stirring occasionally, for 45 minutes until the onions are browned and very tender. Add water as needed if the onions seem to be sticking. Turn the heat to low if the onions turn dark brown before they are very tender. Onions are ready to cool and refrigerate at this point. Makes about 2 cups.

Variation: For onion "marmalade," add the vinegar and cook for another 15 minutes. Spoon into a glass container. Store in the refrigerator for up to 10 days.

Green Onion Spread & Dip Base

Spread on tortillas as a base for raw vegetable sandwiches or add mayonnaise and sour cream to transform the spread into a dip.

- 8 ounces cream cheese, softened
- 2 tablespoons sour cream
- 3 green onions
- 2 tablespoons chopped parsley
- Few drops of lemon juice
- Salt to taste

Beat the cream cheese with the sour cream until smooth.

Slice the green stems of the onions. If they have large white bulbs, chop and add up to ¼ cup of the white. (Chop and freeze the rest, or set aside for another use.)

Add the green onions, parsley, lemon juice and salt to the cream cheese mixture. Chill in the refrigerator for 30 minutes for flavors to blend. Keeps several days in the refrigerator.

To make a dip, beat in ½ cup additional sour cream or mayonnaise. Makes 9 (1-ounce) servings.

Caramelized Onions with a Balsamic Variation

Taking the Harvest to the Table

Peppers

When to harvest

Picking can be done any time you have something that looks like a pepper. Pick them little or big, green or red, but don't stop picking or the plant will stop producing.

Signs that it is ready

Pick sweet peppers when they are bright green and their skins are firm and shiny. Leave some to ripen an extra few weeks—they will turn red and be much sweeter than younger, green peppers.

When is it too late?

When the peppers get spotty or mushy, it is too late to eat them.

How to harvest

Don't pull or twist the pepper off the plant or you may damage the stems. Cut fruit stems with garden shears to avoid snapping off brittle branches. Harvest peppers over the entire season until the first frost.

Expected yield

From five to ten peppers per plant depending on the variety.

TIPS

KID'S CORNER

Peppers take longer than many other plants to yield, up to several months. Make a project of growing several different varieties of sweet peppers, including bell peppers, pimentos, banana peppers, and Italian frying peppers, or other mild varieties to see which ones ripen first. Taste each pepper at the green stage and at the red stage. Make good notes on harvest and flavor, or prepare a chart—this is valuable information your family can use when it's time to plan next year's garden.

■ *Storage*

Peppers have the best flavor picked fresh and not refrigerated. To keep them for more than two days, refrigerate peppers in plastic bags. Be sure they are dry when you put them in the bag. Red peppers will last about a week in the refrigerator; green ones may last a bit longer. Peppers freeze very well. They lose their crispness, but they keep their flavor for up to three months. To freeze peppers, wash them, then cut out the stem and remove the seeds. Cut the peppers into halves, rings, or strips, and pack them into freezer bags or boxes.

■ *Eat / Don't Eat*

Only the fruit and seeds are edible.

■ *Companion Planting*

Basil has the same general requirements as sweet peppers. Plant peppers near okra, which serve as a windbreak to prevent high winds from tipping or breaking brittle pepper plants.

■ *This 'n' That*

It is believed that pepper can help reduce high blood pressure.

PENNY PINCHER

Sharp or rounded-end children's scissors are very easy to work with among the plants you are pruning or harvesting. Children's scissors are small enough to slip right into your shirt pocket, where you can pop them in and out easily as you go around your garden.

Fire-Roasted Pepper Cream Soup

Beautiful made with red peppers, and delicious if less colorful made with green or yellowish peppers.

- 12 medium sweet, mild red peppers such as bell or banana peppers
- Vegetable oil
- 1 large supersweet onion, chopped
- 3 tablespoons unsalted butter
- 2 garlic cloves, chopped
- 2½ cups chicken broth
- 1 cup half-and-half
- Salt and freshly ground pepper to taste

Prepare a fire in a grill or preheat the oven to 425 degrees. Coat the peppers with vegetable oil. Roast, broil or grill over indirect heat, turning occasionally, for 15 to 20 minutes until the peppers are tender and the skins are blackened in places. Put the peppers into a plastic bag and close the bag. Let stand for 15 minutes. Remove the pepper stems and discard the cores and seeds. Peel the skins.

Sauté the onion in the butter in a large saucepan over medium heat for 8 minutes until tender. Add the garlic and sauté for 2 minutes longer. Add the peppers and broth. Bring to a boil; simmer for 2 to 3 minutes. Add the salt and pepper. Cover and simmer for 5 minutes. Add the cream. Purée the soup in a blender or food processor in batches, or use an immersion blender. Return the soup to the pan and heat through. Makes 4 servings.

Slow-Cooker Peppers & Onions

The classic topping for grilled or fried Italian sausages doesn't heat up the kitchen.

- 2 large onions, sliced into rings
- 6 to 8 mild or medium peppers, seeded and chopped or sliced into rounds
- 1 teaspoon salt
- ¼ cup vegetable oil

Combine the onions, peppers and salt in the slow cooker; mix well. Add the vegetable oil and stir to coat the onions and pepper. Cook on low for 1½ hours. The vegetables cook slowly at first, then need frequent stirring. Add a few tablespoons of water if the mixture seems to be sticking. Continue cooking for up to 3 hours until peppers reach desired consistency. The peppers and onions will keep in the refrigerator for several days. Makes 2 to 3 cups.

Fire-Roasted Pepper Cream Soup

Italian Roast Pepper Salad

Sweet peppers from the garden get a dose of garlic and just a hint of lemon, olive oil and oregano. The skins of banana peppers and Italian frying peppers are tender and can be left on, but bell pepper skins should be removed.

6 to 8 large sweet peppers, such as banana peppers, Italian frying peppers or bell peppers
3 garlic cloves, minced
2 tablespoons lemon juice
4 tablespoons olive oil
½ teaspoon minced fresh or dried oregano
Salt and freshly ground pepper to taste

Coat the peppers with oil or nonstick cooking spray. Roast at 425 degrees, turning once or twice to roast all sides, for 20 minutes until blackened in places. Cut off the stem and cut out the seeds. Slice the peppers into strips.

(To peel the tough skin from bell peppers, transfer the peppers to a plastic bag and fold or twist the bag to close. Let stand for 15 minutes. Peel off the skin.)

Combine the peppers, garlic, lemon juice, olive oil, oregano, salt and pepper in a bowl and mix well. Serve at room temperature or chilled. Peppers keep in the refrigerator for up to 3 days. Makes 6 to 8 servings.

Sauté of Zucchini & Peppers

Homegrown zucchini and peppers can release a lot of liquid in the skillet. A sprinkle of flour turns the liquid into a sauce.

2 tablespoons vegetable or olive oil
2 tablespoons butter
3 small zucchini, shredded
4 sweet peppers, cut into slices
2 mild green peppers, cut into slices
A sprig of fresh thyme
A 2-inch sprig of rosemary
Salt and freshly ground pepper to taste
1 tablespoon flour

Heat the oil and butter in a large skillet over medium heat. Add the zucchini, peppers, thyme, rosemary, salt and pepper. Sauté until the vegetables are tender and are beginning to release their juices. Sprinkle with the flour and continue cooking. The flour will absorb the juices and form a "sauce." Remove the rosemary. Serve hot. Makes 6 servings.

Italian Roast Pepper Salad

"Just Chiles" Green Chile Salsa

Top eggs, burritos, or steak with this mild pepper salsa. Turn it into a classic salsa verde by adding several roasted or grilled tomatillos and puréeing the mixture.

6 to 8 long, mild peppers such as banana, Anaheim or Italian frying peppers
Vegetable oil
1 teaspoon cumin seed
½ cup chopped onion
2 garlic cloves, minced
1 to 2 tablespoons vegetable oil
1 cup water
Salt to taste

Preheat to oven to 400 degrees. Coat the peppers with oil or nonstick cooking spray. Roast, turning once or twice to roast all sides, for 20 minutes until blackened in places. Peel the skin, cut off the stem and cut out the seeds. Chop the peppers. Toast the cumin seed in a skillet for 3 minutes until fragrant. Grind in a spice grinder or pound in a mortar and pestle.

Sauté the onion and garlic in the vegetable oil in a small skillet over medium-low heat for 8 to 10 minutes until tender. Add the peppers, cumin, water and salt. Cook, uncovered, for 10 minutes. (If the mixture seems thin, cook until more of the liquid has evaporated.) Chill the salsa in the refrigerator. Makes 1½ to 2½ cups.

Hot Pepper Paste

Preserve those peppers longer by turning them into paste. A spoonful adds just a touch of heat to sauces, salsa, soups, ground beef filling, sour cream topping, and more.

4 large mild peppers
4 small hot peppers
3 tablespoons water
1 teaspoon salt
1 teaspoon sugar
2 tablespoons vegetable oil or olive oil

Cut off the stems and discard the cores of the peppers. Cut out the seeds of the hot peppers for a milder heat level. Cut the peppers into chunks.

Combine the peppers, water, salt, sugar and oil in a food processor or blender until finely chopped.

Transfer the mixture to a saucepan. Bring to a simmer over low heat. Simmer for up to 1 hour, stirring frequently, until the mixture is reduced to a thick paste. Check often, as the mixture may begin sticking to the pan as it thickens. Spoon into a small jar or sealable plastic container. Keeps in the refrigerator for up to 1 week. Freeze for longer storage. Makes ¾ cup.

Chile con Queso

Homemade chile con queso is good enough to make a meal of, with tortilla chips and vegetables for dipping. Or use it as a sauce with tacos or baked potatoes. You can sauté the peppers along with the onions and garlic, rather than roasting them. The taste and texture will be a little different, but you may find the time savings is worth the trade-off.

3 to 5 long mild or medium peppers such as banana peppers, Italian frying peppers, poblanos or Anaheim chiles
Vegetable oil
1 small onion, chopped
1 garlic clove, minced
2 tablespoons butter
2 medium tomatoes, chopped
½ cup crema, crème fraiche, heavy cream or sour cream
¼ cup water
8 ounces Monterey Jack cheese, shredded or very thinly sliced

Preheat the oven to 400 degrees. Coat the peppers with oil or non-stick cooking spray. Roast, turning once or twice to roast all sides, for 20 minutes until blackened in places. Peel the skin, cut off the stem and cut out the seeds. Chop the peppers.

Sauté the onion and garlic in the butter in a skillet over medium-low heat for 8 to 10 minutes until tender. Add the tomatoes. Cover and cook for about 5 minutes until the tomatoes are softening and breaking up.

Turn the heat to low. Add the crema, water and cheese and mix well. Cook, stirring, until hot. Remove the pan from the heat. Cover and let stand for 5 minutes until the cheese is melted. Makes 16 servings.

Refrigerator Pickled Peppers

Choose sweet or hot peppers according to your taste. Sweet peppers are good for snacking and vegetable trays. Pickled hot peppers can be rinsed and used like a fresh chile. If there's extra space in any of the jars, add green beans, carrots, or onions.

- 2 pounds sweet or hot peppers
- 12 black peppercorns
- 6 to 8 teaspoons coriander seeds
- 3 or 4 bay leaves
- 1 small red onion, thinly sliced
- 6 to 8 garlic cloves, cut into halves
- 2½ cups vinegar
- 2½ cups water
- 1 tablespoon salt
- 3 tablespoons to ⅓ cup sugar, to taste

Leave small peppers whole, cutting a small slit near the stem so flavorings will penetrate. Cut large peppers into strips. (Hot peppers can also be cut into halves lengthwise and seeds and ribs removed.)

Pack the peppers, peppercorns, coriander seeds, bay leaves, onion, and garlic into three or four clean glass pint jars. Heat the vinegar, water, salt and sugar in a small saucepan; cook, stirring, until the sugar dissolves.

Pour the vinegar mixture over the peppers. Top with a lid and secure with a ring. Refrigerate for at least 1 week before using. The peppers will keep for several months in the refrigerator. Makes 3 to 4 pints.

Fresh Pepper Lentil Salad

Pepper season seems to arrive all of a sudden. This potluck or supper salad uses some of that bounty for a satisfying result.

- 3 sweet banana peppers, Italian frying peppers or 1 large bell pepper
- 3 tablespoons minced cilantro or parsley
- 2 tablespoons minced mint, optional
- 3 cups cooked brown lentils, cooled
- 1 small garlic clove, minced
- 2 tablespoons olive oil
- Juice of 1 lemon (about 3 tablespoons)
- 1 teaspoon salt
- ½ teaspoon freshly ground pepper
- ½ teaspoon ground coriander
- Crumbled feta cheese, optional

Remove the stem, core and seeds from the peppers and chop them. Combine them in a medium bowl with the cilantro, mint and lentils. Add the garlic, olive oil, salt, pepper, lemon juice and coriander and mix well. Sprinkle with the cheese. Makes 6 to 8 servings.

Jamaican Pepper Papaya Sauce

Papaya and cucumber or squash thicken this sauce and tame its heat. Peaches make a good local substitute for papaya.

- 1 medium cucumber or yellow squash, peeled and deseeded, shredded
- 3 carrots, peeled, shredded or ground
- 6 hot peppers, stems cut off, deseeded (optional), shredded or ground
- 1 small very ripe papaya or 3 peaches, peeled, deseeded, shredded or puréed
- 2 teaspoons salt
- 1 to 2 teaspoons brown sugar
- ⅓ cup vinegar
- 1 cup water

Combine the cucumber, carrots, peppers, papaya, salt, sugar, vinegar, and water in a medium nonstick or other coated or nonreactive pan. Bring to a boil over medium-high heat, reduce the heat to low, and cover. Simmer for 30 minutes until very tender. Sample the mixture for texture. Fill small bottles or jars with the sauce. (Use jars if the texture is thick and spoonable.) Keeps for months in the refrigerator.

For a thinner, pourable sauce, add another ¼ cup water and bring to a boil. For a smooth texture, purée the sauce in batches. Fill jars as directed. Makes 2 to 3 cups.

Taking the Harvest to the Table

Potatoes

When to harvest

New potatoes are really baby potatoes and command a BIG price in the grocery store. Dig these valuable little potatoes as soon as you see blooms on the vine. Dig an entire plant whenever you need new potatoes, either by removing the plant or by harvesting all the baby potatoes and putting the plants back in the soil and watering well. The potatoes increase by one size every few days.

Signs that it is ready

Potatoes are ready for the main harvest when the vines have turned brown, indicating that the potato skins are mature.

When is it too late?

After the potato foliage dies, you can leave the potatoes in the ground for a few weeks, but dig them if you are expecting a heavy frost, as freezing ruins potatoes, or a warm, wet spell.

How to harvest

Dig carefully, starting from the outside and getting down under the potatoes so that you don't cut or scratch them. Use a garden fork rather than a spade to reduce the chances of cutting into the potatoes.

Expected yield

You can expect almost five pounds of full-size potatoes per square foot.

TIPS

KID'S CORNER

One way plants are classified is by what part we eat (like root crops). List the different categories you can think of, and then all the plants under that category. What else is in the category with potatoes? For how many of the plants can you eat two parts? And how do you think potatoes form seeds?

■ *Storage*

The ideal storage spot for a potato is dark, humid but not damp, and well ventilated. Potatoes do best at a stable 40°F. Colder than that and they become sweet as the starch converts to sugar. Below freezing, the potatoes will be ruined. Warmer than 40°F and they tend to re-sprout. Do not wash the potatoes before storing, and do not pile them more than a foot deep. Keep them in the dark so they don't turn green.

■ *Eat / Don't Eat*

Only the potato tubers are edible.

■ *Companion Planting*

Plant potatoes near broccoli, sweet corn, scarlet runner bean, nasturtium, or marigold; horseradish helps potatoes be more resistant to diseases. Don't plant potatoes near melons, sunflowers, tomatoes, or pumpkins.

Mel says...

Select potato varieties for Square Foot Gardening carefully. Some early varieties produce potatoes only in the lowest six inches. Look for a late-season variety—if the tag doesn't tell you, log onto www.squarefootgardening.com and visit the regional forums, where fellow gardeners can share their potato growing success tips.

Polish Potato Salad

- 3 medium potatoes, peeled, cut into bite-size pieces
- 2 carrots, peeled
- 3 eggs, hard-boiled, chopped
- ½ medium apple, peeled, chopped
- 2 kosher dill pickles, chopped
- 1½ cups fresh or thawed peas
- ¼ cup sliced green onion
- ¼ cup low-fat mayonnaise
- 1 tablespoon prepared mustard
- 2 tablespoons low-fat sour cream
- 2 teaspoons lemon juice
- ¼ teaspoon ground nutmeg
- Salt and freshly ground pepper to taste

Cook the potatoes in boiling salted water for 3 minutes. Add the carrots and cook for 4 to 5 minutes longer until both are tender. Drain them well. Combine them with the eggs, pickles, peas, apple and onions.

Combine the mayonnaise, sour cream, lemon juice, mustard, nutmeg, salt and pepper in a small bowl and mix well. Spoon or pour over the vegetable mixture. Mix gently. If the dressing seems thick, add a little whipping cream or vegetable oil. Let the salad marinate for 30 minutes before serving. Makes 6 to 8 servings.

Wasabi Smashers

- 10 new potatoes
- Salt to taste
- 2 teaspoons wasabi paste
- ¾ cup half-and-half
- 5 tablespoons butter

Cook the potatoes in boiling salted water for 20 minutes until tender. Drain well. Mash the potatoes with a potato masher. Whisk the wasabi into the half-and-half until well blended. Add the butter and wasabi mixture to the potatoes and mix well. Season with salt. Makes 4 to 6 servings.

Polish Potato Salad

Crisp Roast Potatoes

Roast potatoes are ready to eat in 25 minutes. Leave them in longer if you like a deep brown, crisp exterior.

6 to 8 round white or gold potatoes (about 1 pound), peeled or not
¼ cup vegetable oil
Salt and freshly ground pepper to taste
1 teaspoon minced rosemary

Preheat the oven to 400 degrees. Cut the potatoes into chunks. Boil in salted water for 3 to 4 minutes until the outside is tender. Drain, then shake the potatoes roughly in the pan or colander; roughing up the outside is key to a crisp roast potato.

Toss the potatoes with the oil, salt, pepper and rosemary. Spread them in a single layer on a roasting pan. Roast for about 25 minutes, turning once, until the potatoes are golden brown outside and tender inside. Makes 4 servings.

Skin-On Potato Chips

Butter adds a deep, rich flavor to potato chips. If you use butter, be sure to keep the oil temperature at about 300 degrees so it won't burn.

2 cups vegetable oil
1 stick (8 tablespoons) butter, optional
4 fist-size potatoes
Seasoned salt
Garlic powder, optional

Heat the oil and butter to 300 degrees in a saucepan or deep-fryer. (A higher temperature will burn the butter.) If you're using just oil, heat it to 350 degrees.

Cut the potatoes into very thin slices with a mandoline or in a food processor fitted with the thin slicer blade.

Fry the potatoes in batches without crowding for 4 to 5 minutes until they are golden and there are no more little bubbles around them. Drain on paper towels. Sprinkle with seasoned salt and garlic powder. Makes 4 to 6 servings.

Crisp Roast Potatoes

Pepper & Potato Salad

The salad takes on a Mexican flavor when lime juice is used in place of white wine vinegar.

Shallot Vinaigrette

1 shallot, minced
3 tablespoons white wine vinegar or fresh lime juice
3 tablespoons olive oil
½ to 1 teaspoon salt
¼ teaspoon cayenne or freshly ground pepper

Salad

2 pounds red or other new potatoes, sliced or cut into bite-size pieces
Salt
3 mild banana or other sweet peppers, roasted, chopped, or 2 (4-ounce) cans chopped green chiles
3 green onions, sliced
⅓ cup chopped fresh parsley

Combine the shallot, vinegar, olive oil and salt and pepper in a blender or food processor. Process until the mixture is puréed.

Cook the potatoes in boiling salted water for 8 minutes or until tender. Drain and rinse. Combine the potatoes, chiles, green onions and parsley in a medium bowl. Pour the dressing over the vegetable and mix well. Serve warm or at room temperature. Makes 4 to 6 servings.

Baked Red Potato & Cheese Casserole

2 pasilla or ancho chiles
2 pounds large red potatoes, cut into bite-size pieces
¼ cup crumbled feta cheese
½ cup grated or shredded romano cheese
1 teaspoon salt
3 tablespoons vegetable oil
½ cup half-and-half
2 tablespoons snipped chives or 2 green onions, sliced

Preheat the oven to 350 degrees. Remove the stems from the chiles. Slit them open and cut or scrape out the seeds. Cut the chiles into thin slivers. Combine the chiles, potatoes, cheeses, salt, vegetable oil and half-and-half in a bowl and mix well. Spoon or pour into a greased baking dish. Cover with foil and bake for 45 minutes to 1 hour until the potatoes are tender. Sprinkle with chives. Makes 4 to 6 servings.

Sausage & Mushroom Potato Salad

8 small to medium potatoes, about 1½ pounds, cut into slices
1 to 1½ pounds sweet Italian sausage
¼ cup red wine
1 pound sliced mushrooms
¼ cup olive oil
1 teaspoon fresh lemon juice
1 teaspoon hot red pepper sauce
3 sliced green onions
⅓ cup chicken broth
⅓ cup white wine
1 tablespoon Dijon mustard
⅓ cup olive oil
Salt and freshly ground pepper to taste

Cook the potatoes in boiling salted water for 8 minutes or until tender. Drain well.

Prick the sausages with a fork and fry, turning once or twice, over medium heat for 10 minutes. Drain the grease from the skillet. Add the wine and fry for another 5 minutes or until the sausages are cooked through. (Or bake the sausages at 350 degrees for 15 minutes, add the wine, and bake for 15 minutes longer.)

Combine the sausages with the potatoes in a large bowl.

Sauté the mushrooms in the olive oil in a medium skillet over medium-high heat for 5 minutes until they release their liquid and most of it evaporates. Add the lemon juice and hot pepper sauce. Add to the potatoes and sausages along with the green onions. Combine the broth, wine, mustard, oil, salt and pepper in a jar with a tight-fitting lid or a bowl with a whisk or fork. Shake or whisk to combine. Pour the dressing over the salad and mix well. Makes 4 to 6 servings.

Taking the Harvest to the Table

Chard & Friends

When to harvest

Mustard, chard, and kale can be cut for salads as soon as the leaves are a useful size, about two to three inches. For mustard greens, that's about twenty-one days. Plants mature in about fifty-five days. Turnip greens are ready to cut when they are four to six inches long.

Signs that it is ready

Chard is ready any time after leaves reach three inches. Mature greens of chard, kale, and mustard are palm-size or larger. Turnip greens are ready at four inches.

When is it too late?

Turnip greens can be harvested even after the turnip develops. Kale benefits from a light frost. A hard frost will finish off mustard greens.

How to harvest

Harvest chard and kale leaves from the outside of the plant. Cut turnip greens individually or in clumps. Turnip greens can also be harvested along with the turnips.

Expected yield

Eight chard plants will provide enough chard for a family of four for several months until frost. Plant different colors of chard for a nice variety.

TIPS

KID'S CORNER

Look closely at a plant of greens or chard. Where is the seed? If you can't see it, can you guess where it might be? Make a list of plants in the garden that are similar in this way. Make another list of plants with very obvious seeds. Here are some plants that may be on one list or the other.

Corn
Potato
Radish
Cabbage
Lettuce
Pepper
Tomato
Pumpkin
Seedless watermelon

■ *Storage*

Chard, kale and mustard can be left growing in the garden because their flavor improves with the frost. Kale can survive a hard freeze, but chard and mustard cannot. Cut them off when a freeze below 28ºF is predicted.

■ *Eat / Don't Eat*

Both stems and leaves of chard are edible. Kale and mustard leaves are edible, but tough stems should be removed. All parts of the turnip plant are edible.

■ *Companion Planting*

Chard, especially the varieties with colorful stems, look great with dill and strawberries in a corner of the garden. Kale likes to be with radishes and dill.

Mel says...

Many garden-variety greens are edible during two stages. When they're young and tender, they can be eaten fresh in salads. After a few more days in the garden, they mature and develop a chewier texture that is tamed by cooking.

Greek Greens Slices

Health researchers are looking closely at the rural Greek tradition of a pie of seven greens as a possible explanation for Greek longevity. For simple preparation, make it in a traditional pie shape in a shell of phyllo layers, or shape it into a twist-top "paper bag" for an attractive presentation.

1 pound mixed greens (mustard greens, watercress, arugula, kale, chard, sorrel, dandelion), chopped or torn
1 (10-ounce) box frozen spinach, thawed, squeezed dry (about 1 cup)
2 medium leeks, minced
1 cup sliced mushrooms
1 cup sliced green onions
1 teaspoon minced hot or mild pepper
⅓ cup olive oil
1½ cups crumbled feta cheese
1½ cups shredded kefalotyri, Parmesan or pecorino cheese
2 eggs
1 cup chopped fresh dill
¼ cup chopped fresh basil or fennel fronds
16 phyllo sheets
Olive oil for brushing

Heat 1 cup water in a large skillet or soup pot and add the greens. Cook for 5 minutes until wilted and tender; drain, pressing out the water. Chop the greens. Add the spinach and mix well.

Preheat the oven to 375 degrees. Sauté the leeks, mushrooms, onions and pepper in the oil for 8 to 10 minutes until the leeks are soft. Add the greens and cook for 3 minutes. Stir in the cheeses, eggs, dill and fennel. Shape the pie as desired, using the directions below. Bake the pie for 40 to 45 minutes. (The bag and the pie shapes bake at different rates, so watch for browning at the edges of the phyllo.) Let stand 15 minutes then slice and serve. Can also be served at room temperature or cold.

Makes 6 to 8 servings.

To bake in a baking dish, oil a 1½-quart round or square glass casserole dish. Layer 8 phyllo sheets over it, brushing each layer with oil and staggering the sheets to cover the dish. Fill with the greens mixture, pressing it into the corners. Cover with 8 more phyllo sheets. Fold the phyllo over the filling to cover it, or trim the edges, and bake as directed.

To shape into a "paper bag," layer 8 phyllo sheets in a circular pattern on a work surface with the center ends overlapping but outer ends staggered like a pinwheel. Make sure all 8 pieces overlap in the center so they can support the filling. Brush the phyllo with oil. Spoon the greens mixture into the center. Pull up edges and twist top shut. Transfer to baking sheet. Brush with oil. Bake as directed.

Greek Greens Slices

Sautéed Greens

Any greens, including beet tops and overgrown arugula, can become a garlicky, spicy side dish.

- 1 pound mixed greens
- Salt
- 3 garlic cloves, chopped
- ¼ cup olive oil
- 1 hot pepper, minced, or ½ teaspoon red pepper flakes
- Olive oil for drizzling

Cook the greens in boiling salted water to cover for 5 minutes until tender; drain. Squeeze the water from the greens. Chop them if desired.

Sauté the garlic in the olive oil in a medium skillet over medium heat for 1 minute. Add the hot pepper and sauté for 1 minute. Add the greens and a little water to the skillet. Raise the heat to high and cook, stirring, for 3 to 4 minutes until the water has evaporated. Drizzle with additional olive oil to taste and season with salt. Makes 4 small servings.

Southern-Style Greens

It's traditional to use a mixture of collard, mustard and turnip greens for a balanced flavor that combines sharp and mellow greens and a texture that includes both firm and tender greens.

- 2 smoked ham hocks
- 3 tablespoons vegetable oil
- 1 small dried red pepper
- 2 garlic cloves, chopped, or ½ teaspoon garlic powder
- 2 pounds collard greens, mustard greens or turnip greens, torn
- 6 cups water

Fry the ham hocks in the oil in a very large pan over medium heat for about 20 minutes until some of their fat is rendered and they are brown. Add the pepper and garlic and cook for 1 minute. Add the greens and mix well to coat with oil. Add the water and mix well. Cover and bring to a boil, pushing the greens down occasionally, until all the greens are under the cooking liquid. Uncover and simmer for 35 minutes until the greens are tender.

Retrieve the ham hocks, pull the meat from the bones, and chop the meat, discarding the bones and fat. Return the meat to the pot. Chop the greens and return to the cooking liquid. Serve the greens with the cooking liquid. Makes 8 servings.

Sautéed Greens

Mustard Green or Kale Salad with Shallot Dijon Vinaigrette

Young leaves of kale and mustard greens can be chopped for salad. You may have to harvest a few a day for several days to get enough.

Shallot Dijon Vinaigrette

½ cup vegetable oil
3 tablespoons white wine vinegar
½ teaspoon Dijon mustard
3 tablespoons chopped shallots
1 teaspoon salt

Salad

4 medium red potatoes
2 big handfuls young kale or mustard greens, tough central portion removed if necessary, chopped
4 tomatoes, cut into wedges

For the vinaigrette, combine the oil, vinegar, mustard, shallots and salt in a bowl and mix well with a whisk.

For the salad, cut the potatoes into ¼-inch slices and cook in boiling salted water for 7 to 9 minutes until cooked through; drain and rinse. Combine the potatoes with half of the dressing in a bowl. Arrange the potatoes, greens and tomatoes on a platter or in a serving bowl. Drizzle with additional vinaigrette. Makes 6 servings.

Chard & Bean Sauté

Mix up a quick sauté of chard and cannellini beans—you can substitute white beans—for a fast side dish or meatless main dish. Smoked paprika (pimentón) added just before the wine adds another layer of flavor.

2 garlic cloves, minced
1 tablespoon olive oil
8 ounces chard, torn or chopped
2 tablespoons dry white wine
½ teaspoon Italian seasoning or chopped fresh oregano, thyme and basil
1 (15-ounce) can cannellini beans, rinsed and drained
1 tablespoon lemon juice
Salt and freshly ground pepper to taste

Sauté the garlic in the olive oil in a skillet over medium heat for 1 minute. Add the chard and cook, stirring, for 5 minutes until it wilts. Add the wine and Italian seasoning and cook until the wine evaporates. Add the beans and mix well. Cook for 5 minutes until the beans are heated through. Add the lemon juice, salt and pepper and mix well. Makes 2 servings.

Rotini with Garlic, Bacon & Greens

The easy way to chop greens is to bunch a handful together on a cutting board and run a knife through the pile. For more finely chopped greens, cut them again after they've cooked.

1½ pounds mild-flavored greens such as chard, chopped, large stems discarded
6 ounces smoked bacon, chopped
3 tablespoons vegetable oil
1½ cups chopped onion
¼ teaspoon red pepper flakes
6 garlic cloves, chopped
½ cup chicken broth
1 tablespoon wine vinegar or balsamic vinegar
1 pound rotini, cooked
Salt to taste
Grated Parmesan or other hard, aged cheese, optional

Cook the greens in boiling salted water for 2 minutes until softened; drain.

Cook the bacon in a skillet over medium-low heat until crisp. Remove from the skillet. Drain all but 2 tablespoons of the grease. Add the vegetable oil to the skillet. Sauté the onion and pepper flakes over medium-low heat until the onion is tender. Add the garlic, greens and broth. Cook for 5 to 7 minutes until greens are tender. Add the vinegar and salt. Cook for 30 seconds or so until you can smell the vinegar. Toss the greens with the pasta and bacon. Top with Parmesan. Makes 4 to 6 servings.

Roasted Kale Chips

A great conversation starter at a gathering. They don't store well, though, so serve them soon after cooking.

12 kale leaves
2 teaspoons salt
3 tablespoons olive oil

Preheat the oven to 375 degrees. Cut kale into large pieces; cut out the thick stems. Combine salt and oil in a large bowl. Add the kale and mix well. Arrange the kale on baking sheets. Bake for about 15 to 20 minutes until crispy. Thick pieces and the edge near the stem crisp more slowly. Makes 6 servings.

Taking the Harvest to the Table

Squashes

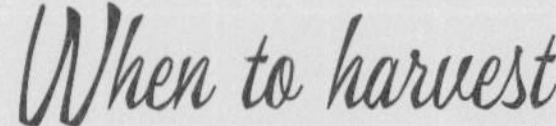

When to harvest

Pick summer squash anytime after they reach about 4 inches long. Leave winter squash on the vine until they are mature. Winter squash will not ripen after picking and do not taste good young.

Signs that it is ready

The tastiest summer squash are the smallest vegetables on the vine. Winter squashes are ready when the stems have shriveled and become brittle.

When is it too late?

Pick summer squash continually or plants will slow and stop production. Pick all squash before frost.

How to harvest

Cut all squash with a sharp knife or garden shears, as pulling or twisting them may damage the plant. Use two hands to hold and cut. When you pick winter squash, cut off a few inches of stem along with the fruit, but do not use the stem as a handle for picking up the squash. Winter squash look like hard tough fruits, but actually they need to be handled carefully.

Expected yield

Summer squash yield so much that you will say, once again, "Why did we plant so many seeds?" Winter squash, depending on the variety, can yield from three to five large squash per plant.

TIPS

KID'S CORNER

Take the idea of an old-fashioned lemonade stand and expand it. When squash are arriving thick and fast, set up a vegetable stand on your street. Do a little research to find out what squash cost in the market, or at a farm stand. Price yours at a cost that seems fair. Can you advertise them as "organic" or "local" to charge more? Will people pay more or less for homegrown vegetables? Will a lower price encourage people to buy? You can learn a lot about business from your squash stand.

■ *Storage*

Acorn squash doesn't store as long as Hubbard or butternut. Ideal storage for winter squash is 60°F with low humidity and good air circulation. Warmer and dry is better than cool and damp. Cure winter squash (but not acorn squash) by bringing them inside where it is warm and dry for two weeks to toughen the skin. Then store in a cooler dry place. **Winter Squash:** Wipe winter squash with a solution of one part chlorine bleach to ten parts water. Dry them and rub them with vegetable oil to help prevent mildew in storage. Cooked winter squash can be frozen in chunks or as purée. **Summer Squash:** Refrigerate unwashed summer squash in a plastic bag for up to four days. Wash and use it before it gets soft. To freeze summer squash, slice it into rounds, cook in boiling water for two minutes, rinse with cold water, drain, and pack into rigid plastic freezer containers or plastic freezer bags. It will keep for up to a year.

■ *Eat / Don't Eat*

All fruits are edible.

■ *Companion Planting*

Radishes will help prevent insects. Let the radishes grow and go to seed. Nasturtiums and tansy will repel squash bugs.

Mel says...

If a winter squash that you are storing begins to look wrinkled at the stem, it's time to eat it or freeze it. To freeze squash, just bake the whole squash until tender, about an hour for a three-pound squash. Let it cool, cut it into halves lengthwise, and scoop out and discard the seeds. Scoop out the flesh and store it in freezer bags or rigid plastic containers. Use it in soups, pies, bread, or in the gnocchi and pancake recipes in this chapter.

Zucchini Parmesan Pancakes

Serve these as a side dish, a breakfast bread, or as the base for creamed chicken or ham.

2 cups grated zucchini
⅓ cup flour
½ teaspoon baking powder
2 eggs, beaten
½ teaspoon salt
¼ teaspoon pepper
¼ cup grated Parmesan cheese
Butter for cooking

Combine the zucchini, flour, baking powder, eggs, salt, pepper and cheese in a bowl and mix well.

Heat 1 tablespoon of butter in a large skillet or griddle on medium heat. For each pancake, pour ¼ cup of the batter into the skillet. Cook for 3 to 5 minutes until the bottom is light brown. Turn the pancakes, cover the skillet, and cook until bottom is browned and the pancakes seem cooked through. Makes 12 to 16 pancakes.

Pattypan Squash Fritters

Pattypan squash, which look like alien space ships, are very mild-flavored. No need to peel them—just cut out the stem. If the squash are large, cut them into halves around the "equator" and cut out the big, hard seeds.

Vegetable oil for frying
2 eggs
½ cup milk
1½ to 2 cups shredded pattypan squash
1 teaspoon vegetable oil
1 cup self-rising flour
¼ teaspoon baking soda
Ketchup
Horseradish sauce

Preheat about half an inch of oil in a deep skillet over medium-high heat to about 350 degrees.

Combine the eggs, milk, squash and oil in a large bowl and mix well. Add the flour, baking soda and salt and mix with a few strokes to combine.

Drop the mixture by tablespoons into hot oil. (In a large skillet, you can cook up to 8 fritters at a time.) Cook until browned on the bottom. Turn and cook the other side until brown. Drain on clean kitchen towels. Serve with ketchup or horseradish sauce. Makes 12 fritters.

Zucchini Parmesan Pancakes

Pumpkin Gnocchi with Sage & Pecans

Be sure to drain and warm the purée to dry it out or it will require up to 2 more cups of flour to reach the right consistency. The mixture holds together without the egg, but it will be lighter if you include it.

- 2 to 3 cups pumpkin purée or butternut squash purée
- 1 egg, optional
- Salt and freshly ground black pepper
- ½ teaspoon freshly grated nutmeg
- 2 cups flour, plus more as needed
- 8 tablespoons (1 stick) butter
- 24 sage leaves
- ½ cup chopped toasted pecans
- ⅔ cup shredded Parmesan cheese

If you're using homemade purée, put it in a strainer and let it drain for at least 30 minutes. Then heat it in a pan over low heat, stirring often, for several minutes to evaporate any excess moisture.

Combine the squash, egg, salt, pepper, nutmeg and enough flour to form a dough that holds together. Knead a few times, adding more flour if needed to make a non-sticky dough.

Form the dough into one or two long rolls about 1 inch in diameter. (At this point, you can dust the dough with flour, wrap it in plastic wrap and refrigerate for later.)

Bring a large pot of water to a boil. Cut off ½-inch segments of dough. (Or pinch off ½-inch pieces, or scoop them with a small spoon.) For true gnocchi, roll the dough pieces over the tines of a fork. Boil 8 to 12 gnocchi at a time. They're ready when they float to the top. Use a slotted spoon to transfer gnocchi to a bowl.

Heat the butter in a sauté pan. Add the sage leaves and pecans. Toast for 1 to 2 minutes until you can smell the sage. Pour over the gnocchi. Top with Parmesan and mix gently. Makes 4 servings.

Pumpkin Gnocchi with Sage & Pecans

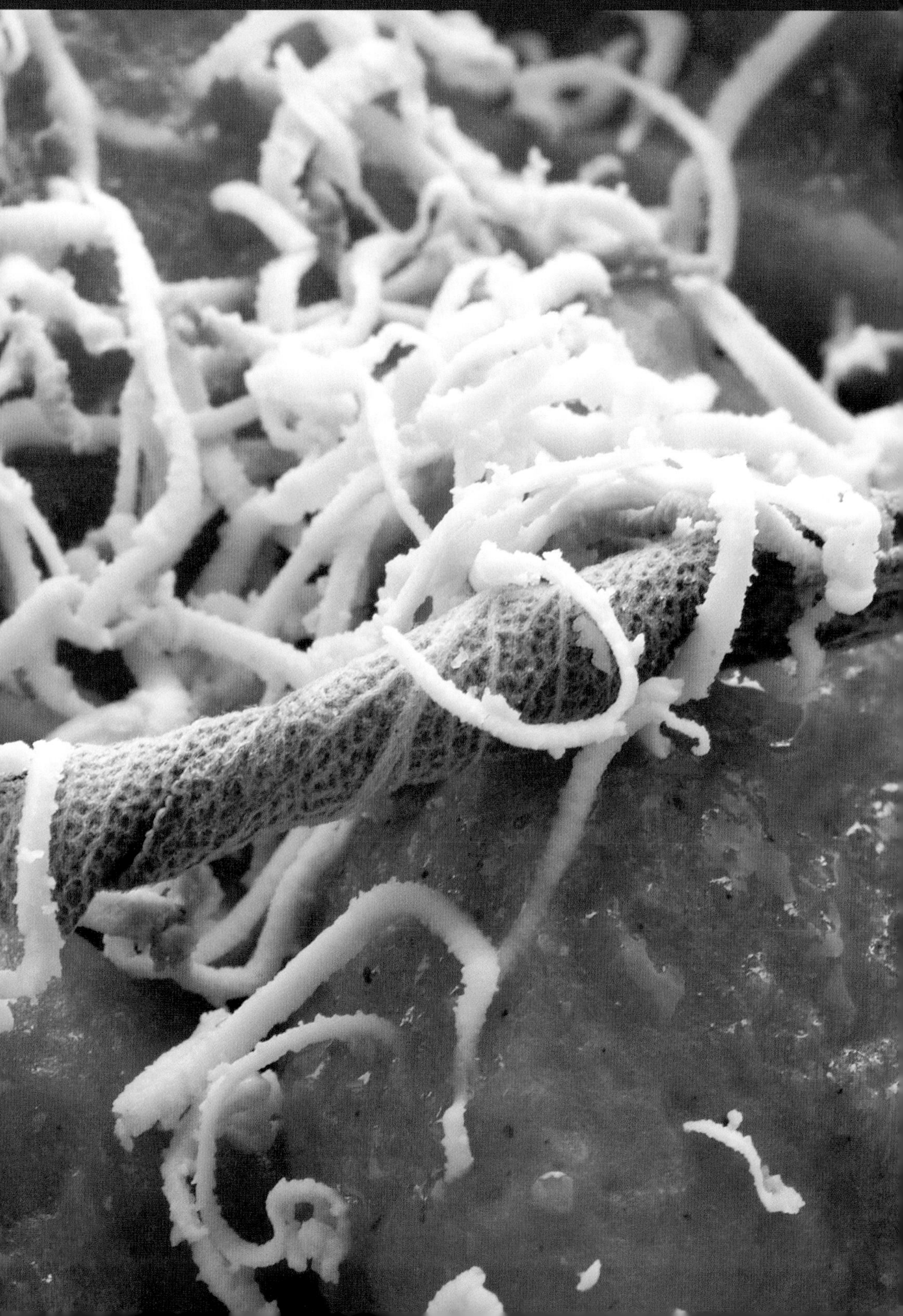

Butterscotch Squash Bread

A departure from the usual squash breads, and unusually good, too.

½ cup vegetable oil
⅔ cup sugar
½ cup brown sugar
2 eggs
1 cup grated yellow squash (1 medium-large squash)
1 teaspoon vanilla extract
1½ cups flour
½ cup oats
1 package instant butterscotch pudding mix (sugar-free is fine)
½ teaspoon salt
½ teaspoon baking soda
¼ teaspoon baking powder
¼ teaspoon cinnamon

Preheat the oven to 350 degrees. Beat the oil and sugars in a large bowl until well mixed and creamy-looking. Add the eggs and mix well. Add the squash and vanilla and mix well.

Combine the flour, oats, pudding mix, salt, baking soda, baking powder and cinnamon in a large bowl and mix well. Make a well in the center. Spoon or pour the squash mixture into the well. Mix until no white streaks of flour remain.

Spoon the mixture into a greased 9- or 10-inch loaf pan. Bake for about 1 hour. Cool in the pan for 10 minutes; remove and cool completely. Makes 1 loaf.

Squash & Crab Soup

A rich, creamy South Carolina-inspired soup.

½ cup (1 stick) butter
1 carrot, grated
1 large onion, minced
1 garlic clove, minced (or ¼ teaspoon garlic powder)
½ teaspoon red pepper flakes
4 medium yellow or pattypan squash, grated (6 to 8 cups)
4 cups (1 quart) water
¼ cup crab, shrimp or lobster soup base
1 pound crabmeat
½ cup all-purpose flour
1 cup milk
1 cup half-and-half
Salt to taste
2 tablespoons snipped chives, optional

Melt the butter in a large soup pan (at least 3 quarts) and sauté the carrot, onion and garlic over medium heat for 8 minutes until tender. Add the pepper flakes and squash and cook for 10 minutes until tender.

Add the crab base and water and mix well. Cover and bring the mixture to a simmer. Add the crab meat. Cook over low heat until heated through. Add more water if it seems too strong or salty (since soup bases vary in strength).

Whisk together the flour and a little of the milk to make a paste. Add the remaining milk and half-and-half and mix well. Add the mixture to the soup.

Cook, stirring, until the soup thickens, but try not to let it boil. Add salt to taste. Garnish with chives to serve. Makes 10 cups.

Cheese-Topped Butternut Tart

This pretty and satisfying entrée is a fun challenge for the project-minded cook. Use either fresh or frozen winter squash. Select a good-quality cheese for the top—the better the cheese, the better the result.

Pecan Crust

¼ cup finely ground pecans or almonds
1 cup all-purpose flour
6 tablespoons very cold butter, cut into bits
¼ cup ice water

Filling and topping

1 cup mashed cooked winter squash
¼ cup heavy cream
1 to 2 tablespoons melted butter
1 large egg
Salt and freshly ground pepper to taste
4 ounces grated aged gouda cheese

For the crust, combine the nut meal and flour in a bowl or in a food processor. Add the butter and cut in or process in pulses to the texture of coarse cornmeal. Add the water and process until the mixture forms a ball. Flatten and cover with plastic wrap. Roll out to fit into an 8- or 9-inch tart pan or springform pan. Press into the pan. Chill for 30 minutes. Bake at 425 degrees for 20 minutes or until golden. Reduce the oven temperature to 375 degrees. Let the crust cool for a few minutes.

Combine the squash with the cream, butter, egg, salt and pepper and mix well or process until smooth. Spoon into the cooled crust.

Spread or sprinkle the cheese over the filling. Bake for 20 to 25 minutes or until filling is puffed and cheese is melted. Makes 6 servings.

Creole Chocolate Squash Muffins

With the addition of cocoa powder, this muffin is closer to an unfrosted cupcake.

- 1 pound (2 to 3 medium) yellow squash
- 2 eggs
- ½ cup melted butter
- ½ cup unsweetened baking cocoa
- ½ cup white sugar
- ½ cup brown sugar
- 3 cups all-purpose flour
- 1 tablespoon plus 2 teaspoons baking powder
- 1 teaspoon salt

Cut the squash into chunks. Cut out any large, hard seeds. Boil, steam or microsteam until very tender. Mash or purée with a potato masher, immersion blender or food processor.

Preheat the oven to 375 degrees. Measure 2 cups of the cooked squash. Add the squash to the eggs in a medium bowl and mix very well. Combine the butter, cocoa, and white sugar. Add to the squash mixture and mix well.

Combine the brown sugar, flour, baking powder and salt in a large bowl. Make a well in center of the dry mixture. Pour or spoon the squash mixture into the well. Mix until no white streaks of flour remain. Spoon the batter into paper-lined or greased muffin tins, filling two-thirds full. Bake for 20 minutes or until muffins test done. Makes about 18 medium muffins.

Pumpkin Pancakes

These versatile pancakes are good with peach jam or maple syrup, or make a meal of them topped with sausage gravy or rolled up with fried ham.

- 4 eggs
- 1 cup half-and-half or whole milk
- 2 tablespoons melted butter
- ¼ teaspoon salt
- ¼ cup sugar
- 1 cup all-purpose flour
- 2 teaspoons baking powder
- 1 cup pumpkin purée
- ¼ teaspoon freshly grated nutmeg
- ⅛ teaspoon cinnamon
- Vegetable oil or butter, for the pan

Combine all ingredients except vegetable oil in a blender and process until smooth. Let stand for at least 15 minutes.

Heat a nonstick griddle, crepe pan or iron skillet with oil over medium heat. Spoon in 2 to 4 tablespoons batter for each pancake—the batter is thinner than traditional pancake batter and will spread. Cook for about 3 minutes until bubbles have formed and burst on the top of the cakes and center seems set. Turn and cook the other side until browned. Makes 24 to 30 pancakes.

Zucchini Lime Bread

If you have trouble getting children to eat and enjoy zucchini, simply bake this bread and call it "Lime Bread." You can make a glaze from lime juice and confectioners' sugar, but the bread is moist and sweet without it.

¾ cup vegetable oil
1½ cups sugar
3 eggs
1 teaspoon vanilla extract
3 cups shredded raw zucchini or yellow squash
Zest and juice of 1 lime
2 cups unbleached flour
1½ teaspoons baking soda
1 teaspoon baking powder
1 teaspoon ground cinnamon
1 teaspoon ground cloves
¼ teaspoon salt

Preheat the oven to 350 degrees. Beat or whisk the oil and sugar until well mixed and creamy-looking. Add the eggs and vanilla and mix well. Stir in the zucchini and lime zest and juice.

Combine the flour, baking soda, baking powder, cinnamon, cloves and salt in a bowl and mix well. Add to zucchini mixture and mix well. Spoon the batter into a greased loaf pan or three greased mini loaf pans. Bake for 40 minutes (small loaves) to 1 hour 15 minutes (large loaf). Cool in the pan 10 minutes, then remove and cool completely. Loaves freeze well. Makes 1 large or 3 small loaves.

Ribbon Salad

A mandoline makes quick ribbons from zucchini and cucumbers. You can also use the slicer blade on a box grater.

2 medium zucchini
1 medium cucumber, peeled
½ cup minced supersweet onion
½ cup torn basil or 2 tablespoons pesto
1 cup torn mint leaves
Zest and juice of 1 lemon
Salt and freshly ground pepper to taste
2 tablespoons peanut oil

Cut the zucchini into quarters lengthwise. Cut out the seeds if they are large. Slice the zucchini into ribbons on a mandoline. Quarter, deseed, and slice the cucumber the same way. Combine the zucchini, cucumber, onion, basil, mint, lemon, salt and pepper and peanut oil in a bowl and mix well. Let stand for 15 minutes for flavors to blend. Makes 4 to 6 servings.

Taking the Harvest to the Table

Tomatoes

When to harvest

Pick tomatoes when they are the color suggested on the seed packet, or slightly before, when the shoulders are not yet fully colored.

Signs that it is ready

Any plump, heavy tomato that is beginning to color can be harvested if absolutely necessary. This is done with store-bought tomatoes. They will continue to ripen after being picked, but they will not have that sweet, fresh, sun-ripened flavor.

When is it too late?

Tomatoes left too long on the vine become mushy.

How to harvest

Treat tomatoes gently, as they are fragile. They should release from the vine with only slight pressure or twisting unless they are not quite ripe. In that case, use scissors to cut the stem.

Expected yield

A full-size vine of indeterminate (constant-bearing) plants typically produces a minimum of fifteen to twenty tomatoes. Over a long season of good weather the yield may be as great as fifty or sixty per plant. Typically, two plants per adult and one per child supply a family's eating and cooking needs for the season.

TIPS

KID'S CORNER

Plan a special "theme" garden. Some ideas include a spaghetti sauce garden, a salsa garden, and a raw salad garden. Tomatoes would be a great addition to any of these "theme" gardens. What else would you put in your special garden? To find out, look up recipes for the dishes you hope to prepare. Make a chart depicting how many plants, and the yield, needed to make one batch of spaghetti sauce, pizza sauce, or salad for your family from your garden.

Storage

Do not refrigerate tomatoes if possible. Pick them just prior to eating and use them at room temperature. Arrange them in one layer and check often to see if they have holes, cracks, or spots. At the end of the season, arrange green tomatoes on shelves or in shallow open containers, in single layers. Don't allow them to touch one another. Then place the containers in an open, airy location away from direct sunlight. Check for ripe fruit every few days and discard any that show signs of spoiling. Freeze ripe whole tomatoes in plastic bags. To use them, break off what you need, and peel them by rubbing the skin off under a stream of hot tap water. Frozen tomatoes are best used in cooked dishes.

Eat / Don't Eat

Eat tomato fruit only, not stems or leaves.

Companion Planting

Don't plant tomatoes with members of the cabbage family (cabbage, cauliflower, broccoli, brussels sprouts), potatoes, corn, or fennel. Good companions are borage, basil, asparagus, gooseberries, chives, onion, parsley, marigold, nasturtium, carrot, and garlic. Tomatoes will protect roses against black spot. Tomatoes are susceptible to diseases transmitted through tobacco, so if you smoke, stop, and don't permit tobacco users in the garden without washing hands first.

Mel says...

Here's another idea for late-season tomatoes. As the first frost approaches, pull up the whole tomato plant and rinse the dirt from the roots. Trim off branches without tomatoes if you wish to make plants more compact. Hang the plant over the rafters in the garage. The tomatoes will gradually ripen, and you can pick and use them. You may still be eating homegrown tomatoes at Christmas time!

Garlic Tomato Pizza & Pasta Sauce

Use this sauce anywhere you'd use tomato sauce, pizza sauce, or pasta sauce. This recipe is adapted from one developed by the Ball jars test kitchen.

½ large onion, chopped
4 garlic cloves, minced
1 tablespoon olive oil
30 medium tomatoes (about 10 pounds), stem end cut out, quartered
¼ cup sliced or torn fresh basil
Lemon juice

Sauté the onion and garlic in the oil in a large pan for 8 minutes over medium-low heat until tender. Add the tomatoes and bring to a boil. Reduce the heat and simmer, uncovered, for 20 minutes, stirring occasionally. Purée in a food processor or blender in batches. Pour the sauce through a strainer to remove the tomato seeds and peel.

Return the sauce to the pan and add the basil. Bring to a boil. Reduce the heat and simmer until the volume is reduced by half, stirring often.

Put the jars into hot water (150 to 200 degrees). When ready to fill, remove the jars from the water. Pour 1 tablespoon of lemon juice into each hot jar. Ladle the simmering sauce into hot jars, leaving ½ inch at the top. Use a clean, damp paper towel to wipe off the rim of the jar. Top with a lid, then fit the band and screw on until tight. Boil for 35 minutes; let cool. Check the seals 12 to 24 hours later. They should not flex up and down when pressed. Makes 3 pints.

Just Enough Pizza Sauce

This recipe yields sauce for a thin layer covering two large (15- to 18-inch) pizzas. If there's any leftover sauce, it keeps for several months in the freezer.

3 large tomatoes or 5 medium tomatoes or 8 Roma tomatoes
1 or 2 garlic cloves, minced
¼ cup olive oil
⅛ teaspoon dried oregano
Salt and pepper to taste

Pour boiling water over the tomatoes in a bowl; let stand 1 minute. Drain and cover with cold water. When tomatoes are cool enough to handle, cut out the core and remove the skin. If you like, cut the tomatoes into halves and squeeze out the seeds. Purée the tomatoes and garlic in a blender or food processor.

Heat the olive oil in a medium skillet over medium-low heat. Add the tomato purée, oregano and salt. Raise the heat to medium-high and cook, stirring often, for 20 minutes, until the mixture is of a thick, spreadable consistency. Add the pepper. Makes 1 to 1½ cups.

Garlic Tomato Pizza & Pasta Sauce

Zucchini Tomato Bake

Use fresh or canned tomatoes for this. The Parmesan in the green can is just fine.

- 3 tablespoons chopped onion
- 3 tablespoons butter or bacon grease
- 2 medium zucchini, sliced
- 2 cups chopped tomatoes
- ½ teaspoon salt
- ¼ teaspoon freshly ground pepper
- ½ grated cup Parmesan
- ½ cup shredded Cheddar cheese

Preheat the oven to 350 degrees. Sauté the onion in the butter in a skillet over medium heat for 8 to 10 minutes until tender. Add the zucchini and tomatoes and cook for 5 minutes until tomatoes lose their "raw" look. Add the salt and pepper. Spoon the mixture into a 1½-quart greased baking dish. Sprinkle with the cheese. Bake for 20 minutes until the cheese is melted. Makes 4 to 6 servings.

Tomato Vegetable Cheese Skillet

Chihuahua cheese mixes with hot pan juices to form a cheese sauce. The mixture is also good piled into a tortilla with chopped cilantro and jalapeño.

- 1 onion, chopped
- 3 tablespoons vegetable or corn oil
- 2 garlic cloves, sliced
- 2 large tomatoes, deseeded, chopped
- 2 medium yellow squash, chopped or diced
- 1 cup corn (cut from 1 to 2 ears)
- Salt and freshly ground pepper to taste
- 1 to 2 sage leaves, crumbled
- 1½ cups shredded Chihuahua or queso blanco cheese (or substitute Monterey Jack)

Sauté the onion in the oil in a skillet over medium-low heat for 8 to 10 minutes until tender. Add the garlic, tomatoes, squash and corn and sauté for 8 minutes until the squash is tender. Turn the heat to low and add the salt, pepper and sage. If the mixture is very watery, drain some of the liquid, or raise the heat and cook until all but a few tablespoons evaporates. Add the cheese and cook, stirring, until the cheese melts. Makes 6 servings.

Zucchini Tomato Bake

Homemade Ketchup

The yield depends on how thick you like your ketchup; the size of the tomatoes; and whether they are juicy "slicer"-type tomatoes, meaty Roma tomatoes, or somewhere in between. Have four pint-size jars ready, just in case.

- 4 pounds (about 16 to 20 medium) tomatoes, stem end cut out, quartered, seeds squeezed out
- 1 or 2 onions, cut into chunks
- 1 or 2 medium sweet red peppers, cored, deseeded, quartered
- 1½ cups white vinegar or cider vinegar
- 1 cup brown sugar
- 2 teaspoons salt
- 2 teaspoons dry mustard
- ½ teaspoon whole allspice berries
- ½ teaspoon whole cloves
- Pinch of red pepper flakes or 1-inch segment of dried red pepper
- 1 cinnamon stick, broken

Grind, process or purée the tomatoes, onions and peppers in blender or food processor, working in batches. Pour the mixture into a large pan. Add the vinegar, sugar, salt and mustard. Put the allspice, cloves, pepper and cinnamon into a tea ball or small cotton bag, or tie them up in cheesecloth or other clean kitchen cloth. Add to the pan.

Bring the mixture to a boil over medium heat. Reduce the heat to low and simmer, uncovered, for 40 minutes, or until the volume is reduced by half. (Or cook it to your preferred consistency and strength.)

Remove the spices. Put the jars into hot water (150 to 200 degrees). When ready to fill, remove the jars from the water. Ladle or pour the ketchup into the jars, leaving ½ inch at the top. Use a clean, damp paper towel to wipe off the rim of the jar. Top with a lid, then fit the band and screw on until tight. Boil jars for 10 minutes; let cool. Check the seals 12 to 24 hours later. They should not flex up and down when pressed. Makes 2 to 3 pints.

Green Tomato BLT with Basil Mayo

Make sure the tomatoes are truly green tomatoes—any red parts can be too soft to fry properly.

1 cup basil leaves
⅔ cup mayonnaise
2 tablespoons fresh lemon juice
2 teaspoons Dijon mustard
12 slices bacon
3 large green tomatoes, cut into 12 slices
¾ cup flour
½ cup yellow cornmeal
Salt and freshly ground pepper
1 egg, beaten
Oil, for shallow frying
1 cup torn or sliced arugula
8 slices white or wheat sandwich bread

For the basil mayonnaise, purée the basil, mayonnaise, lemon juice and mustard in a blender until smooth. Chill in the refrigerator.

Fry the bacon and drain, or keep the drippings for frying the tomatoes.

Spoon half the flour onto a plate or waxed paper. Combine the other half of the flour with the cornmeal, salt and pepper. Arrange the flour, egg and cornmeal mixture in a row on a work surface. Dip each green tomato slice into the flour, then egg, then cornmeal mixture, coating thickly. Pat the coating on so it will adhere. Fry in hot oil for 2 minutes on each side; drain.

Make sandwiches by spreading bread with mayonnaise, then layering green tomato and bacon. Top with arugula and another slice of bread. Makes 4 servings.

Roasted Onion & Green Tomato Salad

Add this combination of tangy green tomatoes plus sweet roasted onions to your salad repertoire.

3 large green tomatoes, cut into wedges
1 medium onion, sliced into thin rounds
3 tablespoons olive oil
3 garlic cloves, minced
Salt to taste
1 cup crumbled feta cheese
1 tablespoon minced fresh mint
1 tablespoon fresh lemon juice
1 tablespoon balsamic or other mild vinegar
¼ cup torn fresh basil leaves
1 to 2 tablespoons olive oil
Salt and freshly ground pepper

Preheat the broiler, or heat the oven to 500 degrees. Combine the tomatoes, onions, olive oil, garlic and salt in a bowl and toss to coat. Spread the tomato mixture on a broiler pan or roasting pan. Broil or roast for 15 to 25 minutes, stirring and turning once or twice, until the vegetables are tender and browned on the edges.

Combine the feta, mint, lemon juice, vinegar, basil and olive oil in a salad bowl. Add the roasted vegetables and salt and pepper to the bowl and mix well. Serve warm or at room temperature. Makes 6 servings.

Tomato Onion Ginger Salad

A tomato salad with Indian flavors is a change of pace for tomato season.

2 tablespoons lime juice
½ teaspoon sugar, optional
Salt to taste
¼ cup vegetable oil
2 large ripe tomatoes
2 inches of fresh ginger, peeled
½ red onion, thinly sliced
1 tablespoon chopped fresh mint (3 or 4 sprigs) or cilantro

Combine the lime juice, sugar, salt and vegetable oil in a small bowl with a whisk or a fork, or in a jar with a tight-fitting lid. Whisk or shake to combine.

Slice the tomatoes and arrange on a serving platter. Arrange the onions over the tomatoes. Cut the ginger into thin slices, then into sticks. Arrange the ginger over the onions. Drizzle the dressing over the vegetables. Sprinkle with the mint. Makes 4 servings.

Bread & Tomato Salad

Use stale homemade bread or rustic, coarse-textured "country" bread from a bakery.

- 6 slices country bread
- 2 large tomatoes, chopped
- 1 medium cucumber, cut into quarters and sliced
- ½ cup chopped supersweet onion
- 1 cup chopped flat-leaf parsley
- 1 garlic clove, minced
- ¼ cup fresh lemon juice (about 2 lemons)
- ¼ cup olive oil
- Salt and freshly ground pepper to taste

Toast the bread in an oven or toaster at low heat until very dry and hard. Cut into cubes or break into bite-size pieces. Set aside. Combine the tomatoes, cucumber, onion and parsley in a large bowl. Combine the garlic, lemon juice, olive oil, salt and pepper in a small bowl with a fork or whisk, or in a jar with a tight-fitting lid. Whisk or shake to blend. Pour over the vegetables. Shortly before serving, add the bread and mix well. Let stand 15 minutes for the bread to soften slightly. Makes 6 servings.

Chopped Tomato & Cucumber Salad

In high tomato season, you may find yourself making this salad often. Switch between lemon juice and lime juice for variety. This recipe makes a generous batch, and is a good choice for potlucks because it's safe and delicious at room temperature.

- 3 medium tomatoes
- 2 medium to large cucumbers
- 1 supersweet onion, chopped
- ⅓ cup minced fresh mint
- ½ cup chopped fresh flat-leaf parsley
- ¼ cup lemon or lime juice
- ¼ cup vegetable oil
- 2 tablespoons white wine vinegar
- Salt and freshly ground pepper

Cut the tomatoes horizontally and squeeze out the seeds. Cut out the cores. Chop the tomatoes. Peel the cucumbers if desired. Cut into quarters lengthwise and cut out the seeds. Slice the cucumbers.

Combine the tomatoes, cucumbers, onions, mint and parsley in a large salad bowl. Pour on the lime juice, vegetable oil and vinegar. Sprinkle with the salt and pepper. Toss to blend. Let stand for 20 minutes for flavors to blend. Refrigerate for up to 12 hours. Drain before serving. Makes 6 to 8 servings.

Appendix

Planting Grids

SPRING

Use this guide to lay out your spring plant selections—remember, a different crop in each square foot. Include some spring flowers such as pansies in each 4×4.

Planting Grids

SUMMER

Use this guide to lay out your summer plant selections—remember, a different crop in each square foot. Include some summer flowers such as dwarf marigolds in each 4×4.

Planting Grids

FALL

Use this guide to lay out your fall plant selections—remember, a different crop in each square foot. Include some fall chrysanthemums in each 4×4.

Planting Schedule for Continuous Harvest Crops

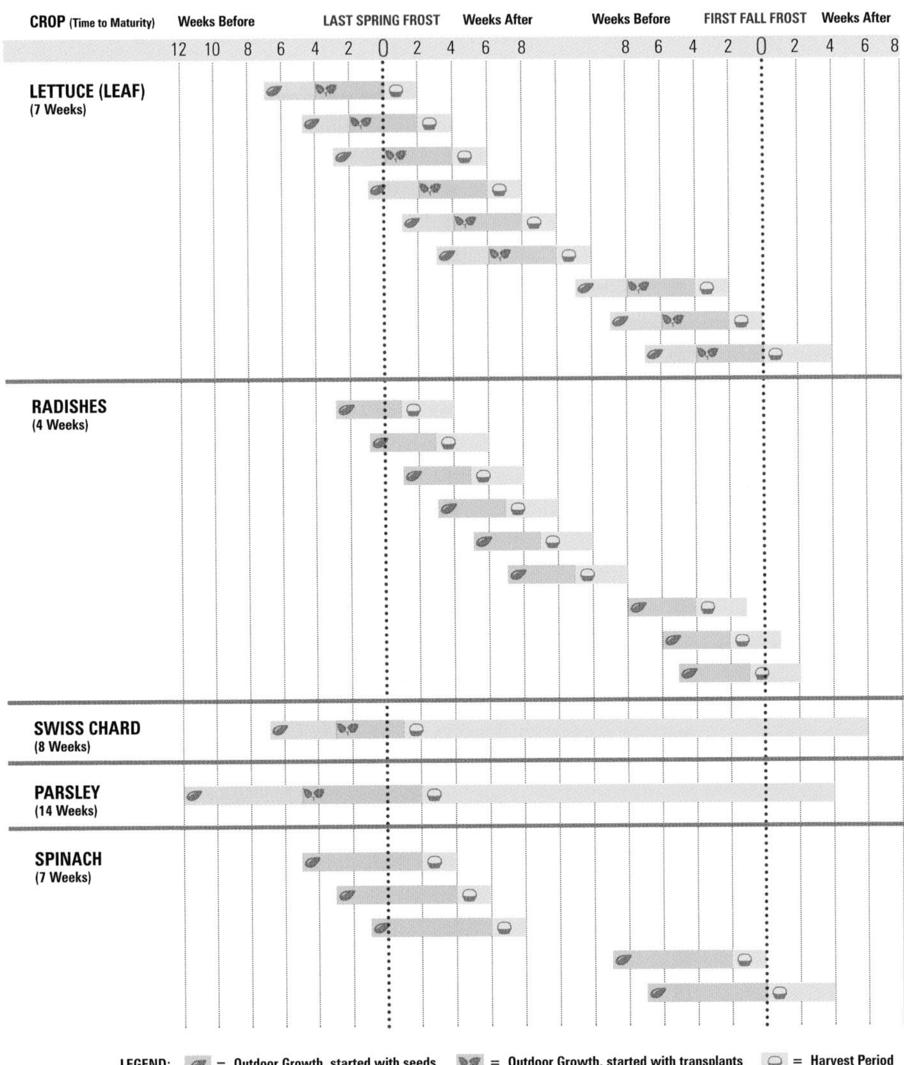

LEGEND: = Outdoor Growth, started with seeds = Outdoor Growth, started with transplants = Harvest Period

= Indoor Growth, started with seeds

Planting Schedule for Continuous Harvest Crops

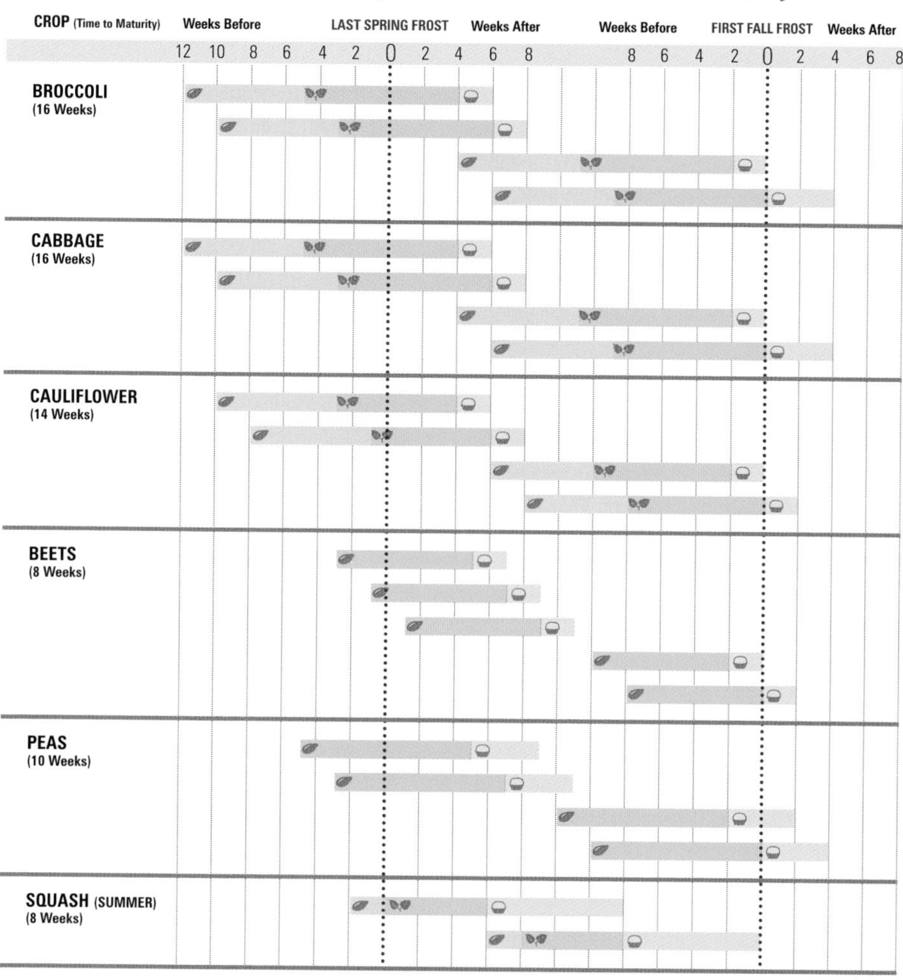

Planting Schedule for Continuous Harvest Crops

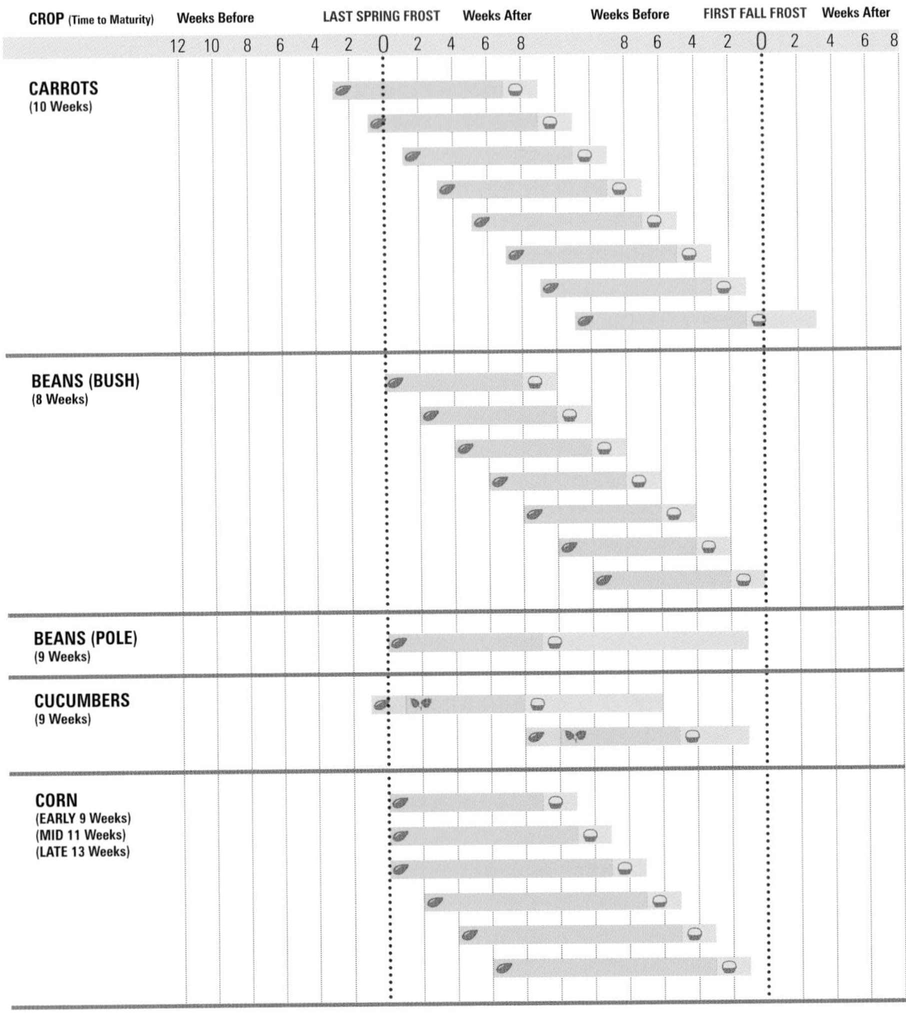

Planting Schedule for Continuous Harvest Crops

LEGEND: = Outdoor Growth, started with seeds; = Outdoor Growth, started with transplants; = Harvest Period; = Indoor Growth, started with seeds

Plant Spacing

Extra Large
1 Plant
Placed 12 inches apart:

Broccoli

Cabbage

Pepper

Large
4 Plants
Placed 6 inches apart:

Leaf Lettuce

Swiss Chard

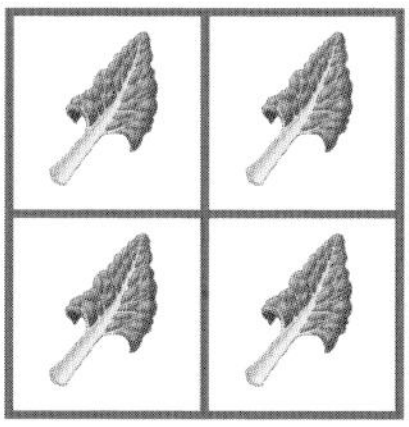

Marigold

Medium
9 Plants
Placed 4 inches apart:

Bush Bean

Spinach

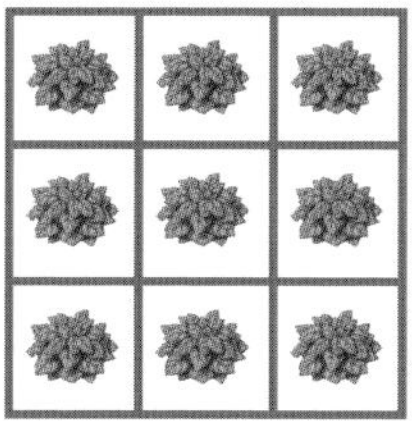

Beet

Small
16 Plants
Placed 3 inches apart:

Carrot

Radish

Onion

Index

Appetizers & snacks
Brunch Asparagus Pick-Ups, 20
Chile con Queso, 123
Cucumber Sandwiches, 62
Eggplant Fries, 72
Green Bean Munchers, 33
Green Onion Spread & Dip Base, 114
Grill-Smoked Baba Ghanoush, 72
Herb Cheese-Stuffed Snow Peas, 106
Herb Toastlets, 78
Herbed Eggplant Spread, 70
Herbed Goat Cheese Spread, 80
Hot Asparagus Cheese Fingers, 23
"Just Chiles" Green Chile Salsa, 122
Roasted Kale Chips, 141
Skin-On Potato Chips, 130
Strawberry Lemonade & Freezer Pops, 98

Arugula
Arugula & Chervil Salad, 84
Arugula & Potato Salad, 88
Green Tomato BLT with Basil Mayo, 159
Persian Herbs & Greens Oven Omelet, 89

Asparagus
Asparagus Frittata, 20
Asparagus Wild Rice Salad, 18
Brunch Asparagus Pick-Ups, 20
Crisp Sesame Ginger Asparagus, 23
Fresh Asparagus Snow Pea Slaw, 22
Grilled Asparagus, 22
Hot Asparagus Cheese Fingers, 23
Pasta with Peas, Asparagus & Cream, 107
Roasted Asparagus with Cherry Tomatoes, 18

Bacon
Brunch Asparagus Pick-Ups, 20
Crisp Cool Broccoli Salad, 38
Green Tomato BLT with Basil Mayo, 159
Main Dish Spinach Salad with Smoky Bacon Dressing, 91
Rotini with Garlic, Bacon & Greens, 141

Basil
Basil-Scented Zucchini & Pea Sauté, 107
Classic Ratatouille, 70
Eight-Herb Butter Pasta, 78
Fresh Asparagus Snow Pea Slaw, 22
Green Tomato BLT with Basil Mayo, 159
Make-Your-Own Salade Niçoise with Basil Vinaigrette, 28

Beans, dried
Chard & Bean Sauté, 140
Fresh Pepper Lentil Salad, 124

Beans, pole
Pole Beans with Garlic & Sweet Onions, 32

Beef
Cabbage Rolls, 44
Sesame & Orange-Scented Beef & Broccoli, 36
Stir-Fried Beef & Green Beans, 30

Berries
Berry Crunch Coffeecake, 98
Blueberry Fool, 96
Fresh Strawberry Bread, 99
Strawberry Lemonade & Freezer Pops, 98

Beverages
Cucumber Ginger Limeade, 65
Strawberry Lemonade & Freezer Pops, 98
Watermelon Wave, 94

Breads
Bread & Tomato Salad, 161
Butterscotch Squash Bread, 148
Creole Chocolate Squash Muffins, 150
Fresh Strawberry Bread, 99
Pattypan Squash Fritters, 144
Pumpkin Pancakes, 150
Zucchini Lime Bread, 151
Zucchini Parmesan Pancakes, 144

Broccoli
Broccoli & Red Pepper Salad with Herb Cream, 40
Broccoli in Garlic Brown Butter, 40
Creamy Chicken Broccoli Skillet, 38
Crisp Cool Broccoli Salad, 38
Horseradish Broccoli Sandwich Topper, 41
Italian Chopped Vegetable Salad for a Crowd, 41
Sesame & Orange-Scented Beef & Broccoli, 36

Cabbage
Blue Cheese Slaw, 46
Cabbage Baked with Feta, 48

Crunchy Carrot Slaw, 54
Cumin Cabbage & Rice, 49
Fish Tacos & Cucumber Cilantro Slaw, 46
Noodles & Browned Cabbage, 48
Two-Cheese Cabbage & Ham Salad, 49

Carrots
Carrot Timbale with Herb Crisp, 52
Crunchy Carrot Slaw, 54
Jamaican Pepper Papaya Sauce, 125
Polish Potato Salad, 128
Quick Balsamic Carrots, 52
Savory Carrot Olive Sandwich Spread, 54
Spiced Carrot Relish or Salad, 57
Sweet Peanut Carrot Spread, 57
Thai Roasted Vegetables, 56
Wintry Carrots Baked in Cream, 56

Cauliflower
Italian Chopped Vegetable Salad for a Crowd, 41

Cheese
Arugula & Chervil Salad, 84
Baked Red Potato & Cheese Casserole, 132
Blue Moons, 62
Cabbage Baked with Feta, 48
Cheese-Topped Butternut Tart, 149
Chile con Queso, 123
Creamy Chicken Broccoli Skillet, 38
Crisp Green Beans with Blue Cheese & Walnuts, 33
Eggplant & Tomato Pasta Sauce, 68
Fried Halloumi Salad with Caper Vinaigrette, 90
Garlic & Rosemary Baked Feta, 112
Greek Greens Slices, 136
Grilled Pepper & Eggplant Sandwiches, 73
Herb Cheese-Stuffed Snow Peas, 106
Herbed Goat Cheese Spread, 80
Hot Asparagus Cheese Fingers, 23
Pumpkin Gnocchi with Sage & Pecans, 146
Roasted Onion & Green Tomato Salad, 160
Tomato Vegetable Cheese Skillet, 156
Two-Cheese Cabbage & Ham Salad, 49
Watermelon Mint Feta Salad, 96
Zucchini Parmesan Pancakes, 144
Zucchini Tomato Bake, 156

Chicken
Asian Chicken Lettuce Wraps, 86
Chicken Herb Sauce for Polenta or Pasta, 81
Creamy Chicken Broccoli Skillet, 38
Tarragon Chicken Salad, 81

Condiments
Chile con Queso, 123
Cucumber Sauce, 60
Green Onion Spread & Dip Base, 114
Homemade Ketchup, 158
Horseradish Broccoli Sandwich Topper, 41
Hot Pepper Paste, 122
Jamaican Pepper Papaya Sauce, 125
"Just Chiles" Green Chile Salsa, 122
Slow-Cooker Peppers & Onions, 118
Spiced Carrot Relish or Salad, 57

Corn
Tomato Vegetable Cheese Skillet, 156

Cucumbers
Asian Cucumber Salad, 64
Blue Moons, 62
Bread & Butter Refrigerator Pickles, 65
Chopped Tomato & Cucumber Salad, 161
Creamy Cucumber & Radish Salad, 60
Cucumber Ginger Limeade, 65
Cucumber Sandwiches, 62
Cucumber Sauce, 60
Fish Tacos & Cucumber Cilantro Slaw, 46
Italian Chopped Vegetable Salad for a Crowd, 41
Jamaican Pepper Papaya Sauce, 125
Ribbon Salad, 151
Tuna & Cucumber Pasta Salad, 64

Dessert
Berry Crunch Coffeecake, 98
Blueberry Fool, 96
Butterscotch Squash Bread, 148
Creole Chocolate Squash Muffins, 150
Fresh Strawberry Bread, 99
Mixed Melons with Ginger Lime Syrup, 99
Strawberry Lemonade & Freezer Pops, 98
Watermelon Cake with Watermelon Frosting, 94
Zucchini Lime Bread, 151

Dips & spreads
Chile con Queso, 123
Cucumber Sauce, 60
Green Onion Spread & Dip Base, 114
Grill-Smoked Baba Ghanoush, 72

Herbed Eggplant Spread, 70
Herbed Goat Cheese Spread, 80
Savory Carrot Olive Sandwich Spread, 54
Sweet Peanut Carrot Spread, 57

Dressings & sauces
Basil Vinaigrette, 28
Caper Vinaigrette, 90
Chive Vinaigrette, 112
Cucumber Sauce, 60
Eggplant & Tomato Pasta Sauce, 68
Garlic Tomato Pizza & Pasta Sauce, 154
Green Goddess Dressing, 80
Herb Cream, 40
Hoisin Sesame Cooking Sauce, 86
Jamaican Pepper Papaya Sauce, 125
Just Enough Pizza Sauce, 154
Lemon Blue Cheese Vinaigrette, 49
Lime Honey Dressing, 84
Peanut Coconut Sauce, 56
Rice Vinaigrette, 54
Rosemary Lemon Vinaigrette, 22
Sesame Ginger Vinaigrette, 23
Sesame Orange Sauce, 36
Shallot Dijon Vinaigrette, 140
Shallot Vinaigrette, 132

Eggplant
Classic Ratatouille, 70
Creole Shrimp-Stuffed Eggplant, 73
Eggplant & Tomato Pasta Sauce, 68
Eggplant Fries, 72
Grilled Pepper & Eggplant Sandwiches, 73
Grill-Smoked Baba Ghanoush, 72
Herbed Eggplant Spread, 70
Mediterranean Eggplant Salad, 68

Eggs, brunch & breakfast
Asparagus Frittata, 20
Berry Crunch Coffeecake, 98
Brunch Asparagus Pick-Ups, 20
Butterscotch Squash Bread, 148
Carrot Timbale with Herb Crisp, 52
Creole Chocolate Squash Muffins, 150
Fresh Strawberry Bread, 99
Make-Your-Own Salade Niçoise with Basil Vinaigrette, 28
Mixed Melons with Ginger Lime Syrup, 99
Pattypan Squash Fritters, 144
Persian Herbs & Greens Oven Omelet, 89
Polish Potato Salad, 128
Pumpkin Pancakes, 150
Zucchini Lime Bread, 151
Zucchini Parmesan Pancakes, 144

Entrées
Asian Chicken Lettuce Wraps, 86
Cabbage Rolls, 44
Cheese-Topped Butternut Tart, 149
Creamy Chicken Broccoli Skillet, 38
Creole Shrimp-Stuffed Eggplant, 73
Cumin Cabbage & Rice, 49
Greek Greens Slices, 136
Main Dish Spinach Salad with Smoky Bacon Dressing, 91
Pea Risotto, 102
Sausage & Mushroom Potato Salad, 133
Sesame & Orange-Scented Beef & Broccoli, 36
Stir-Fried Beef & Green Beans, 30
Two-Cheese Cabbage & Ham Salad, 49

Fish & seafood
Creole Shrimp-Stuffed Eggplant, 73
Fish Tacos & Cucumber Cilantro Slaw, 46
Make-Your-Own Salade Niçoise with Basil Vinaigrette, 28
Squash & Crab Soup, 148
Tuna & Cucumber Pasta Salad, 64

Fruit
Berry Crunch Coffeecake, 98
Blueberry Fool, 96
Crisp Cool Broccoli Salad, 38
Cucumber Ginger Limeade, 65
Escarole Salad with Lemon Pear Dressing, 88
Fresh Strawberry Bread, 99
Jamaican Pepper Papaya Sauce, 125
Mixed Lettuces, Mango & Avocado with Lime Honey Dressing, 84
Mixed Melons with Ginger Lime Syrup, 99
Strawberry Lemonade & Freezer Pops, 98
Sweet Peanut Carrot Spread, 57
Watermelon Cake with Watermelon Frosting, 94
Watermelon Mint Feta Salad, 96
Watermelon Wave, 94

Garlic
Broccoli in Garlic Brown Butter, 40
Garlic & Chive Mashed Potatoes, 112
Garlic & Rosemary Baked Feta, 112
Garlic Tomato Pizza & Pasta Sauce, 154
Pole Beans with Garlic & Sweet Onions, 32
Rotini with Garlic, Bacon & Greens, 141
Whole Roasted Garlic, 111

Green beans
- Crisp Green Beans with Blue Cheese & Walnuts, 33
- Green Bean Munchers, 33
- Make-Your-Own Salade Niçoise with Basil Vinaigrette, 28
- Refrigerator-Pickled Beans, 31
- Roasted Green Bean & Potato Salad, 32
- Roasted Green Beans, 30
- Stir-Fried Beef & Green Beans, 30

Greens
- Chard & Bean Sauté, 140
- Greek Greens Slices, 136
- Mustard Greens or Kale Salad with Shallot Dijon Vinaigrette, 140
- Roasted Kale Chips, 141
- Rotini with Garlic, Bacon & Greens, 141
- Sautéed Greens, 138
- Southern-Style Greens, 138

Ham & sausage
- Sausage & Mushroom Potato Salad, 133
- Southern-Style Greens, 136
- Two-Cheese Cabbage & Ham Salad, 49

Herbs
- Arugula & Chervil Salad, 84
- Carrot Timbale with Herb Crisp, 52
- Chicken Herb Sauce for Polenta or Pasta, 81
- Chive Vinaigrette, 112
- Chopped Tomato & Cucumber Salad, 161
- Crunchy Pea & Peanut Salad, 106
- Eight-Herb Butter Pasta, 78
- Garlic & Chive Mashed Potatoes, 112
- Garlic & Rosemary Baked Feta, 112
- Greek Greens Slices, 136
- Green Goddess Dressing, 80
- Herb Cheese-Stuffed Snow Peas, 106
- Herb Toastlets, 78
- Herbed Eggplant Spread, 70
- Herbed Goat Cheese Spread, 80
- Persian Herbs & Greens Oven Omelet, 89
- Pumpkin Gnocchi with Sage & Pecans, 146
- Ribbon Salad, 151
- Tarragon Chicken Salad, 81
- Watermelon Mint Feta Salad, 96

Lettuce & mixed greens
- Arugula & Chervil Salad, 84
- Arugula & Potato Salad, 88
- Asian Chicken Lettuce Wraps, 86
- Escarole Salad with Lemon Pear Dressing, 88
- Fried Halloumi Salad with Caper Vinaigrette, 90
- Make-Your-Own Salade Niçoise with Basil Vinaigrette, 28
- Mixed Lettuces, Mango & Avocado with Lime Honey Dressing, 84
- Persian Herbs & Greens Oven Omelet, 89
- Two-Cheese Cabbage & Ham Salad, 49

Nuts
- Cheese-Topped Butternut Tart, 149
- Crisp Cool Broccoli Salad, 38
- Crisp Green Beans with Blue Cheese & Walnuts, 33
- Crunchy Carrot Slaw, 54
- Crunchy Pea & Peanut Salad, 106
- Persian Herbs & Greens Oven Omelet, 89
- Pumpkin Gnocchi with Sage & Pecans, 146
- Savory Carrot Olive Sandwich Spread, 54
- Sweet Peanut Carrot Spread, 57
- Tarragon Chicken Salad, 81

Olives
- Italian Chopped Vegetable Salad for a Crowd, 41
- Make-Your-Own Salade Niçoise with Basil Vinaigrette, 28
- Savory Carrot Olive Sandwich Spread, 54

Onions
- Caramelized Onions with a Balsamic Variation, 114
- Green Onion Spread & Dip Base, 114
- Grilled Sweet Onion Packets, 111
- Italian Chopped Vegetable Salad for a Crowd, 41
- Pole Beans with Garlic & Sweet Onions, 32
- Roasted Onion & Green Tomato Salad, 160
- Slow-Cooker Peppers & Onions, 118
- Tomato Onion Ginger Salad, 160

Parsley
- Italian Chopped Vegetable Salad for a Crowd, 41

Pasta & noodles
- Asian Chicken Lettuce Wraps, 86
- Chicken Herb Sauce for Polenta or Pasta, 81
- Eggplant & Tomato Pasta Sauce, 68
- Eight-Herb Butter Pasta, 78
- Garlic Tomato Pizza & Pasta Sauce, 154
- Noodles & Browned Cabbage, 48
- Pasta with Peas, Asparagus & Cream, 107
- Pumpkin Gnocchi with Sage & Pecans, 146

Rotini with Garlic, Bacon & Greens, 141
Tuna & Cucumber Pasta Salad, 64

Peas
Basil-Scented Zucchini & Pea Sauté, 107
Blue Cheese Slaw, 46
Creamy Pea or Sugar Snap Soup, 104
Crunchy Pea & Peanut Salad, 106
Herb Cheese-Stuffed Snow Peas, 106
Pasta with Peas, Asparagus & Cream, 107
Pea Risotto, 102
Polish Potato Salad, 128
Snow Pea or Sugar Snap Stir-Fry, 104

Peppers & chiles
Blue Cheese Slaw, 46
Chile con Queso, 123
Classic Ratatouille, 70
Fire-Roasted Pepper Cream Soup, 118
Fresh Pepper Lentil Salad, 124
Grilled Pepper & Eggplant Sandwiches, 73
Hot Pepper Paste, 122
Italian Chopped Vegetable Salad for a Crowd, 41
Italian Roast Pepper Salad, 120
Jamaican Pepper Papaya Sauce, 125
"Just Chiles" Green Chile Salsa, 122
Pepper & Potato Salad, 132
Refrigerated Pickled Peppers, 124
Sauté of Zucchini & Peppers, 120
Slow-Cooker Peppers & Onions, 118

Pickles & relishes
Bread & Butter Refrigerator Pickles, 65
Polish Potato Salad, 128
Refrigerated Pickled Peppers, 124
Refrigerator-Pickled Beans, 31
Spiced Carrot Relish or Salad, 57

Pizza
Garlic Tomato Pizza & Pasta Sauce, 154
Just Enough Pizza Sauce, 154

Potatoes
Arugula & Potato Salad, 88
Baked Red Potato & Cheese Casserole, 132
Crisp Roast Potatoes, 130
Garlic & Chive Mashed Potatoes, 112
Make-Your-Own Salade Niçoise with Basil Vinaigrette, 28
Mustard Greens or Kale Salad with Shallot Dijon Vinaigrette, 140
Pepper & Potato Salad, 132
Polish Potato Salad, 128
Roasted Green Bean & Potato Salad, 32
Sausage & Mushroom Potato Salad, 133
Skin-On Potato Chips, 130
Thai Roasted Vegetables, 56
Wasabi Smashers, 128

Radish
Creamy Cucumber & Radish Salad, 60
Escarole Salad with Lemon Pear Dressing, 88

Red pepper
Broccoli & Red Pepper Salad with Herb Cream, 40

Rice
Asparagus Wild Rice Salad, 18
Cabbage Rolls, 44
Cumin Cabbage & Rice, 49
Pea Risotto, 102

Salad
Arugula & Chervil Salad, 84
Arugula & Potato Salad, 88
Asian Cucumber Salad, 64
Asparagus Wild Rice Salad, 18
Blue Cheese Slaw, 46
Blue Moons, 62
Bread & Tomato Salad, 161
Broccoli & Red Pepper Salad with Herb Cream, 40
Chopped Tomato & Cucumber Salad, 161
Creamy Cucumber & Radish Salad, 60
Crisp Cool Broccoli Salad, 38
Crunchy Carrot Slaw, 54
Crunchy Pea & Peanut Salad, 106
Escarole Salad with Lemon Pear Dressing, 88
Fresh Asparagus Snow Pea Slaw, 22
Fresh Pepper Lentil Salad, 124
Fried Halloumi Salad with Caper Vinaigrette, 90
Italian Chopped Vegetable Salad for a Crowd, 41
Italian Roast Pepper Salad, 120
Main Dish Spinach Salad with Smoky Bacon Dressing, 91
Make-Your-Own Salade Niçoise with Basil Vinaigrette, 28
Mediterranean Eggplant Salad, 68
Mixed Lettuces, Mango & Avocado with Lime Honey Dressing, 84
Mustard Greens or Kale Salad with Shallot Dijon Vinaigrette, 140
Pepper & Potato Salad, 132
Polish Potato Salad, 128

Ribbon Salad, 151
Roasted Green Bean & Potato Salad, 32
Roasted Onion & Green Tomato Salad, 160
Sausage & Mushroom Potato Salad, 133
Spiced Carrot Relish or Salad, 57
Tarragon Chicken Salad, 81
Tomato Onion Ginger Salad, 160
Tuna & Cucumber Pasta Salad, 64
Two-Cheese Cabbage & Ham Salad, 49
Watermelon Mint Feta Salad, 96

Sandwiches & wraps
Asian Chicken Lettuce Wraps, 86
Brunch Asparagus Pick-Ups, 20
Cucumber Sandwiches, 62
Fish Tacos & Cucumber Cilantro Slaw, 46
Green Tomato BLT with Basil Mayo, 159
Grilled Pepper & Eggplant Sandwiches, 73
Herb Toastlets, 78
Horseradish Broccoli Sandwich Topper, 41
Savory Carrot Olive Sandwich Spread, 54
Sweet Peanut Carrot Spread, 57

Soups
Creamy Pea or Sugar Snap Soup, 104
Fire-Roasted Pepper Cream Soup, 118
Squash & Crab Soup, 148

Spinach
Crunchy Carrot Slaw, 54
Greek Greens Slices, 136
Main Dish Spinach Salad with Smoky Bacon Dressing, 91

Squash, summer
Butterscotch Squash Bread, 148
Creole Chocolate Squash Muffins, 150
Pattypan Squash Fritters, 144
Ribbon Salad, 151
Squash & Crab Soup, 148
Tomato Vegetable Cheese Skillet, 156
Zucchini Lime Bread, 151
Zucchini Parmesan Pancakes, 144

Squash, winter
Cheese-Topped Butternut Tart, 149
Pumpkin Gnocchi with Sage & Pecans, 146
Pumpkin Pancakes, 150

Tomatoes
Bread & Tomato Salad, 161
Chile con Queso, 123
Chopped Tomato & Cucumber Salad, 161
Classic Ratatouille, 70
Eggplant & Tomato Pasta Sauce, 68
Garlic Tomato Pizza & Pasta Sauce, 154
Green Tomato BLT with Basil Mayo, 159
Homemade Ketchup, 158
Make-Your-Own Salade Niçoise with Basil Vinaigrette, 28
Mediterranean Eggplant Salad, 68
Mustard Greens or Kale Salad with Shallot Dijon Vinaigrette, 140
Roasted Asparagus with Cherry Tomatoes, 18
Roasted Onion & Green Tomato Salad, 160
Tomato Onion Ginger Salad, 160
Tomato Vegetable Cheese Skillet, 156
Zucchini Tomato Bake, 156

Vegetarian
Baked Red Potato & Cheese Casserole, 132
Cabbage Baked with Feta, 48
Cheese-Topped Butternut Tart, 149
Cumin Cabbage & Rice, 49
Greek Greens Slices, 136
Noodles & Browned Cabbage, 48
Pea Risotto, 102
Persian Herbs & Greens Oven Omelet, 89
Zucchini Tomato Bake, 156

Watermelon
Mixed Melons with Ginger Lime Syrup, 99
Watermelon Cake with Watermelon Frosting, 94
Watermelon Mint Feta Salad, 96
Watermelon Wave, 94

Zucchini
Basil-Scented Zucchini & Pea Sauté, 107
Italian Chopped Vegetable Salad for a Crowd, 41
Ribbon Salad, 151
Sauté of Zucchini & Peppers, 120
Thai Roasted Vegetables, 56
Zucchini Lime Bread, 151
Zucchini Parmesan Pancakes, 144
Zucchini Tomato Bake, 156

Meet Mel Bartholomew

Despite inventing a brand new, simpler way to garden, and then writing the highest-selling garden book in America, Mel is not a horticulturist and has never had any formal agricultural training, most people are startled to learn.

Mel is a civil engineer. After retirement from his own engineering and consulting company, he took up gardening as a hobby. The only method offered back then was the traditional single-row "victory garden" method, which to an engineer was obviously inefficient, wasteful, and just too much work.

Mel toured the country, asking experts why we use the single-row method for home gardening and being told from Maine to California "…because that's the way we've always done it." For an engineer, that is not a very satisfactory answer. So he decided to invent a new way to garden that is more efficient, easier to do, and more friendly to the environment. He named it Square Foot Gardening. Mel then went on to write that famous book, *Square Foot Gardening*, which sold more than a million copies; hosted a television show on PBS for 5 years; and today presides over a non-profit foundation that encourages every household around the world to have a small garden for producing healthful fresh vegetables that are safe, pure and clean.

Square Foot Gardening is all organic and uses no fertilizers, insecticides, or pesticides. Best of all it requires no heavy tools, no hard work, and there are no weeds!

Read Mel's latest book, *All New Square Foot Gardening*, and you will say as millions of others have, "I can do that!"